VIVA
ESPANA

ROSTERS LTD.

VIVA
ESPANA

EDMUND SWINGLEHURST

ROSTERS LTD

Published by ROSTERS LTD.
60 Welbeck Street, London W1
© Rosters Ltd
ISBN 0 948032 28 6

First Edition 1989

Designed and published by ROSTERS
Typeset by Clear Image,
Printed and bound in Great Britain by Cox & Wyman Ltd, Reading, Berkshire.

Contents

Chapter One:
Getting to know Spain

Costas, castanets and corridas are the clichés of Spain and give a distorting mirror image of one of the most thought provoking countries of present day Europe. A country that is still unknown to most travellers, including those who lie on the beaches of Spain's Mediterranean coasts.

In this book we have tried to give an overall picture of this rich and varied land which has mountain ranges to rival the Alps, the largest plateau in Europe, a Mediterranean and Atlantic coast, green valleys and dry deserts. A land moreover in which a varied mix of peoples have left their imprint; including the Romans, Carthaginians, Visigoths, Moors and Berbers, Basques, Asturians and Galicians, not to mention the ancient Celts and Iberians who were among the original inhabitants. In the course of history all those people have come to form the Spanish people. A nation with one of the most unusual cultures of Europe which the Spanish took across the Atlantic to create the Hispanic world of Latin America.

Sense of isolation

The barrier of the Pyrenees and the Spanish preoccupation with its American colonial empire separated Spain from Europe during the centuries when the nations of that continent were taking on their modern character. This has made Spain something of a mystery for northern Europeans who for centuries have thought of Spain as a backward, reactionary nation trapped in the dark cave of religious intolerance and administrative bureaucracy. A sinister country ruled by fear and with little to offer the enlightened countries of the north.

The ubiquitous Augustus Hare travelling in Spain in 1873 thought the country 'a very concentration of dulness (sic) stagnation and ugliness'. Earlier in the century Edmund Burke described it as 'a whale stranded upon the coast of Europe'.

Unkind words, though there might have been a glimmer of truth in their criticisms for many of the thinking people of Spain were also aware of their country's shortcomings and were already laying the foundations on which a new Spain would arise a hundred years later. Among these were Menendez y Pelayo whose library has been conserved at Santander, Becquer the poet and social satirist from Seville and Angel Ganivet the moral philosopher. Towards the end of the century the intellectual ferment became more agitated with the increasing preoccupation with human values of Alarcon, the author of *The Three Cornered Hat*, and Perez Galdos, the novelist.

A new destiny

During the last decade of the nineteenth century and the first of the 20th when Spain suffered a mortal blow to its pride by the loss of its last colonies in Cuba, Puerto Rico and the Philippines, writers turned more and more to the examination of national life and of human destiny. Among them the eccentric Unamuno, born in Bilbao, who once invited a cow to one of his lectures, and who was exiled for his republican ideals; Pio Baroja, the novelist, and Juan Ramon Jimenez, the poet and author of the children's classic *Platero y Yo*. There was also the great essayist and philosopher Ortega y Gasset who devoted himself to the study of the mystery of the Spanish character. The embodiment of this mystery were the poets. Among them Antonio Machado, whose weaving of the actual realities of the Spanish scene with the world of ideas was the door through which passed Federico Garcia Lorca with his blend of actuality and surrealism which is so typically Spanish and which appears in the work of contemporary Latin American authors.

The expression of a new kind of thinking was also apparent in the visual arts; in the architecture of Gaudi and the work of Miró, Gris and Picasso as well as a host of other lesser known painters who were in the vanguard of the ideas in art which changed the visual sensibility of the world. The cultural upheaval of 19th and 20th century was reflected in Spain by the expression of a growing awareness of the Spanish situation by its people. The Carlist Wars though on the surface a dynastic struggle between the brother of Ferdinand VII and his daughter disguised a deeper rift between conservative and progressive supporters. The suppression and expropriation of religious orders demonstrated the antipathy of the people to centuries of domination by the priesthood. The growing division in the country caused major upsets. In 1873 a Republic was declared but was rapidly replaced by a monarchy under Alonso XII and later Alfonso XIII who, however, abdicated in 1931.

By now the country was deeply split, on the one hand the military and the conservative elements grouped round the fascist style Falange of Jose Antonio Primo de Rivera and on the other the diverse left wing parties. Civil War broke out in July 1936 and the clock was turned back as General Franco and his supporters imposed a military dictatorship which lasted until his death in 1975.

Spanish renaissance

Since then under the wise guidance of King Juan Carlos the long delayed renaissance of Spain has been taking place. The sense of liberation of the Spanish people who have cast off years of constraining manners and mores is as palpable as the industrial activity which is creating new factory areas and housing estates on the fringes of all the major towns.

In this new dynamic society not everything is for the best, much of the architecture is utilitarian, as a result of the rush to provide better accommodation for the working population, traffic congestion in cities is as bad as anywhere else in the world, social manners have lost some of their old world

11

courtesy, and the famous Spanish sense of honour is being dented under the pressures of modern urban life.

Nevertheless much of what was best in Spain still remains, especially in the country regions away from the industrial zones and concrete coastal 'urbanizaciones' that accommodate Spain's 47 million tourists. Spain is a country in transformation. It has all the excitement and dynamism of people and places in a state of transition. Now more than ever is a time to visit it.

Getting there

● Air

Most visitors travel on package holidays or take advantage of the charter aircraft that are used for packages. Fares are lower by charter than on a schedule flight. If you do not have to decide on the date of your holiday in advance you can obtain large reductions for last minute bookings usually advertised in the daily press or in travel agents' windows. Package holidays are limited to certain resorts and by weekly or fortnightly periods and you cannot usually stay over a few days extra. In considering these slight disadvantages you should, however, take into account the enormous saving offered by package holidays. For example a seven-day holiday in high season on the Costa del Sol would cost about £300.00 against about £500.00 if taken independently.

Independent travel away from the coast can be arranged by such specialists as Mundi Color, 276 Vauxhall Bridge Road, SW1X 1BE, 01-826 6021.

● Train

Few people travel by train but it can be fun, and not tiring, if you are heading for a northern resort. London to San Sebastian takes 24 hours with a change of trains in Paris (Gare du Nord to Gare Austerlitz). The most comfortable way to travel is on a Wagons Lits sleeping car. This costs about £165.00 first class return for the fare and about £80.00 for the sleeper but it is worth it.

There are restaurant cars on trains from Paris both to Port Bou (for the Costa Brava) and Hendaye (for the north east coast). There are discounted prices for under 26's, children and senior citizens.

Prices quoted are correct at present but will change. Please check before you go. For advice on all rail fares contact the Thomas Cook Rail Centre on 0733-502530.

● **By car**
If you do not mind driving all the way you can get to Spain with a one night stop along the Le Havre, Paris, Orleans, Bordeaux, Spanish frontier motorway. There is a motorway all the way to the Mediterranean frontier at La Junquera but for north east Spain you leave the motorway at Bordeaux and drive through the flat country of the Landes to Bayonne, near the Hendaye-Irun border post, where you pick up the French motorway which leads on to the Spanish one which goes as far as Bilbao. From Calais to Hendaye is 1058 miles (1700 kilometres).

French motorways are excellent with motorway car and catering services approximately every 20 kilometers and frequent rest areas (Aire) with toilets.

An easier way to take your car to Spain is to put it on the train. French car sleepers go from Paris to Bordeaux, Paris to Biarritz and even Paris to Madrid. The latter leaves Paris at 17.45 arriving Madrid 09.55 throughout the year.

Better still, though you will not see much of the French countryside, is to go by Brittany Ferries from Plymouth to Santander. This costs about £140.00 for car and fare and takes 24 hours, you leave at 0900 have lunch on the Channel and see Ushant just before dinner. If you wake up early enough you will see dawn over the Pyrenees and the Picos de Europa before breakfast.

Documentation

Members of EEC countries, USA, Canada need only their passport in Spain for a stay of less than three months.

If you are a motorist, whether in your own car or a hired one you will need an international driving licence. In your own car you will need a green card insurance and a bail bond

13

which will ensure that you do not get clapped in jail if you have an accident. See the AA about the first and your insurance company or the AA about the second.

Money

You can take travellers cheques in sterling or dollars or in Spanish pesetas, if you use the latter you will not need to worry about the rate of exchange is on any particular day. Alternatively, you can take Eurocheques which can be made out for the amount of pesetas that you need to draw from a bank or to pay for any purchase. Eurocheques require a cheque card issued by the bank that issues the Eurocheque book, and sometimes a passport or other proof of identity. This is often a requirement in all money transactions in Spain.

Credit cards are widely accepted in Spain. The most familiar to Spanish people are American Express, Visa and Access. Cash dispensers are now found more widely but you need to ask your bank for a special Euro number in order to use them.

Getting around in Spain

● Air

Iberia and Aviaco run an extensive network of internal flights and prices are very reasonable, for example you can go from Barcelona to Madrid return for only £107.

● Train

Spanish train services are good but complicated, especially local services which can often be agonisingly slow. Fun though. If you have the time and want to enjoy a kind of Paul Theroux train experience it is worth while putting up with the discomfort of third class travel among the hospitable and gregarious Spaniards.

When booking find out what kind of train you will be travelling on as there are more than a dozen categories beginning with the TEE, Talgo and Ter trains which are fast and comfortable and ending with the semi directo which stops everywhere.

There are also a large number of fares and discounts and special Blue Days (Dias Azules) when there are bargain journeys. Usually you have to queue to buy tickets so it is best to go to a travel agent or the Spanish Railways office, RENFE. RENFE also has many car rail services to all parts of Spain which are useful if you get tired of driving along the long empty roads on the Spanish meseta.

If you want to see Spain by train, and it is the next best thing (some people say better) to driving yourself, a Spanish package train excursion may be the answer. One of these is the Trans Cantabrica across the north of Spain from Leon to El Ferrol on the Galician coast, another is the Al-Andalus across Andalucia.

● Coach
There are good bus and coach services in Spain and the days of rickety old buses filled with peasants and live chickens have gone forever. On the luxury coaches you even get films, air conditioning and toilets, which sometimes make me long for the bad old days.

● Taxis
Cheap enough to encourage you to hail the first to pass whenever you feel tired. Taxi drivers are polite and very helpful. They often know about good places to eat and do not try to push the one owned by their cousin.

Accommodation
● Hotels
Local tourist offices can supply lists of hotels or you can get lists for each region before you start from the Spanish National Tourist Office which is at 57/8 St James Street, London SW14 1LD Tel: 01-499 0901. All hotels in Spain are controlled by the Ministry of Tourism and standards are adhered to rigidly. Also, you will find that the category of a

hotel is based on its general standards of furnishings, service, cleanliness etc. and stars are not awarded simply because the hotel has installed a lift, or a tiny pre-fab shower in order to claim a higher rating. We have not attempted to suggest hotels in all towns but have only mentioned rather special and historical paradors or hotels of an unusually high quality or interest.

● **Paradors**
These government run hotels deserve special mention because they are of very high quality and often situated in historic buildings. They came into being because the Spanish Ministry of Tourism thought it would be a good idea to provide accommodation at places of unusual interest outside the familiar tourist towns. It was a particularly happy idea to situate them in castles, convents, monasteries, noble houses and other historic mansions.

It was not always possible to find ancient buildings and as the demand for parador accommodation has increased many entirely new ones have been built, though in a traditional regional style. Today there are some 80 paradors listed which can be obtained from the Spanish National Tourist office. Since they are intended for travellers who are touring Spain, paradors will not usually accept bookings for more than two or three nights, though if rooms are free you can apply for an extended stay once you arrive. The standard of food at the paradors is excellent and menus usually include specialities of the region in which they are situated.

Food and drink
If you are interested in haute cuisine restaurants Spain can be a disappointment except in the Basque countries, Catalonia, Madrid or along the costas where the density of the tourist population makes expensive international style restaurants viable. Basically Spanish cooking consists of fresh ingredients, well but simply cooked. Most menus feature a long list of fish and shellfish dishes. The following is an imaginary menu such as you might come across in any large town or city.

16

- **Starters – Entremeses** (also found as good tapas)

Alcachofas	– Artichokes
Aceitunas	– Olives
Chipirones en su tinta	– Baby octopus in their own ink
Gambas a la plancha	– Prawns grilled on a hot plate
Huevos flamenco	– Poached eggs with a hot pepper sauce
Calamares fritos	– Fried squid rings
Patatas fritas	– Crisps
Tortilla	– Spanish omelette stuffed with potatoes, onion etc.
Tortilla francesa	– Light fluffy omelette
Jamon Serrano con melon	– Ham, from the Sierras, with melon

- **Main dish**

Arroz a la Valenciana	– A risotto with chicken and shellfish
Arroz a la Cubana	– A risotto with eggs and bananas
Bacalao al pil pil	– A rich stew made with dried cod
Boquerones	– Fresh anchovies (fried)
Besugo al horno	Baked sea bream
Cangrejo con majonesa	– Spider crab with mayonnaise
Centolla	– Crab
Callos a la Madrileña	– Tripe in the Madrid style
Chuletas de cordero	– Lamb chops
Cabrito Asado	– Roast kid
Cochinillo	– Roast sucking pig
Cordero a la Segoviana	– Roast lamb Segovian style
Rapé	– Monk fish
Pez Espada	– Sword fish
Pulpo	– Octopus
Merluzo frito	– Fried hake (whiting?)
Mejillones	– Mussels
Perdiz en escabeche	– Partridge in a marinade
Pimento relleno	– Stuffed pepper
Rabo de Toro	– Bulls tail

17

Sardinas a la parilla   – Grilled sardines
Zarzuela   – Fish stew

● **Desserts**
Albaricoque   – Apricots
Cerezas   – Cherries
Fresas con pana   – Strawberries and cream
Flan   – Creme Caramel
Helado   – Ice cream
Higos   – Figs
Manzana   – Apple
Naranja   – Orange
Platano   – Banana
Torta   – Cake
Uvas   – Grapes

● **Drinks**
Red wine   – Vino tinto
White wine   – Vino blanco
Water   – Agua
Mineral water-fizzy   – Agua mineral con gas
        non-fizzy   – sin gas
Lemonade   – Limonada
Beer   – Cerveza
Coffee with milk   – Café con leche
Tea with lemon   – Té con limon
Fruit juice   – Zumo

The cheeses of Spain

The Spanish cheeses are not well known outside Spain and many of them may not be known outside their own region. Most of them are made by traditional manual methods, not by machinery, and the milk used is often unpasteurised, though this may change now that Spain is a member of the EEC. With their down to earth, country character Spanish cheeses provide an interesting and enjoyable experience for the traveller who is used to the mass produced cheeses of northern Europe. **Manchego** is the best known and most widely distributed cheese. The best of it comes from around

Toledo, Cuenca and Ciudad Rodrigo and as its name implies other places in La Mancha. It is not unlike the Italian Parmesan cheese in texture and sweet richness of flavour, and it also has this cheese's tendency to go rock hard as it matures. This is a quality much admired by Spaniards though it can sometimes cause concern to visitors especially if they find it in a sandwich in which they expected to encounter a filling with a softer texture. In its early stages when newly made the cheese is called fresco (fresh) and when fully mature it is viejo (old). A similar cheese to Manchego is **Grazalemo** which is found in Andalucia especially around Cadiz.

Fresh creamy cheeses are produced in most regions of Spain and may be made of cow, goat or ewe's milk. In Andalucía this kind of cheese is called **Malaga**. It is mostly based on goats milk. All three kinds of milk are used in the similar cheese made in the Seville countryside and in Alicante they also make a soft fresh cheese from curd which has a bland flavour. The green pastures of north west Spain also produce creamy cheeses, these are usually moulded in small individual shapes and called **Quesucos**.

Cheeses with a more solid texture are found in north west Spain especially in Galicia where the local cheese is popularly named after its place of origin, **Queso Gallego**, but also known as **Ulloa**. Other firm textured cheeses come from Aragon, and Leon, and from Badajoz in Extremadura comes a rich, honeycomb coloured cheese called **Serena** which is moulded in esparto grass containers.

Spain has only two veined cheeses one comes from Asturias and is called **Cabrales** which suggests that it is made from goat (cabra) milk, but this is not necessarily so, and the other cheese with less marked veins is **Garmonedo**, which like Cabrales has a strong flavour which is enhanced by a smoking process before it is stored in caves.

In travelling about Spain you may not always find the cheeses under the name we have given, sometimes they may have a regional name. It is better therefore not to worry about the names but to try the one that takes your fancy on the cheese board.

The wines of Spain

Apart from the enjoyment of pre-prandial sherry one of the pleasures of travelling in Spain is the abundance and good value of the wines. These will come on the whole from two great wine producing areas of Spain; La Rioja, which lies south of the Basque country, and Navarre in the Ebro valley and La Mancha.

The vineyards of La Rioja are divided into two areas. Those of the Rioja Alta (Upper Rioja) around the town of Haro and those of Rioja Baja (Lower Rioja) which stretches roughly from Logroño, the capital of the wine country, to Alfaro, down river towards Aragon.

Rioja wines are produced by a large number of bodegas (producers and shippers). These companies which also have their own vineyards, export wine abroad and distribute it throughout Spain and their names soon become familiar to travellers. The ones most commonly found on wine bottles are **Bodegas Franco Españolas**, makers of the very popular semi sweet wine called **Diamante**, and the wines of the **Marques de Riscal**, and the **Marques de Murrieta** whose **Ygay** wines are particularly good. The wine producers of the region are **Bodegas Olarra**, **Bodegas Lan** and **Bodegas Alvases** whose light claret type wine make a delightful summer drink.

To the north of La Rioja the damp climate does not suit the wine vineyards but in the Basque country there is a very distinctive white wine called **Chacoli (Txacoli)**. This is one of the green wines also popularised by the growers of northern Portugal and which can be found from Galicia to Navarre.

The region around Tarragona has been making wine since the time of the Romans and has become an expert at the champagne style wines of San Saduni de Noya. The bottles often carry the names of **Codorniu**, **Casa Freixenet** and **Bodega Torres** which is considered one of the best of the demarcated wine zones of Penedes. When ordering champagne it is as well to remember that a very dry wine is called **brut** and a sweet one **dulce**.

South of Madrid is the La Mancha country with its dry non irrigated agriculture known as **secano.** The grapes here produce a wine with a high alcoholic content, as high as 17%, and the wines are generally rather heavy. The production of wine is considerable and in most restaurants all over Spain the house wine is often **Valdepeñas** which comes from an area on the borders of Andalucia.

On the Mediterranean coast there is also a small wine producing area around Alicante and at Almansa and Benicarlo, all strong red wines typical of southern Spain. There is however one unusual light white wine reminiscent of sherry from around Cordoba. Known as **Montilla** this wine was the subject of strong protest from the people of Jerez when shippers tried to sell it as sherry, so it continues to be called Montilla. It is a most enjoyable wine for those summer days when there is nothing better to do than to sit idly under a tree engaged in conversation with friendly Andalucians.

Sherry, **Jerez**, or as it was once known Xeres, is the indisputable pre-meal drink for anyone who is going to keep their palate clear for the enjoyment of good food. It appears that this drink, like port, owes its importance to the taste of the seventeenth century Englishmen who having discovered it, sent it back in large quantities to England and then, as the Empire grew, throughout the world.

This makes Jerez de la Frontera a kind of pilgrimage centre for everyone who enjoys sherry's many aspects and a very enjoyable day can be spent at the bodegas sampling the fino (dry), amontillado (medium) and oloroso (sweet smelling) sherries of such distinguished bodegas as those of **Domecq**, **Duff Gordon**, **Findlater**, **Garvey**, **Gonzalez Byas**, **Harveys** and others.

Social hours

The Spanish are notorious for their long siesta and late eating and you wonder how they manage to get up as early as they do to go to work. In most Spanish cities they do not go to sleep until three o'clock in the morning, or later, but are astir just as early as the cities of northern Europe. Perhaps it is the long midday break that divides the day up into two parts that enables Spaniards to conserve their energy and to be as lively in the morning as in the hours after midnight. For a visitor

21

the two part day takes a while to get accustomed to. This does not apply to the Costas where the preponderantly foreign population have managed to impose their ideas of daily routine on the environment.

In the real Spain most people will get up in time to go to work at 8.30 am and will start the day with a cup of coffee or chocolate often accompanied by the traditional **churros**, a long sausage shaped batter fried in oil. These are sold in churrerías or even by street stalls where people queue up to watch the churros being extruded from the nozzle of a batter container and dropped into the sizzling tank of oil. Once cooked they are powdered with sugar and if given a horseshoe shape by the cook, they are hooked on to a sliver of wood to be carried home for breakfast. Not everyone breakfasts at home, however, for it is often eaten in a café on the way to work and the coffee is sometimes accompanied by something – a drop of brandy – to stimulate the system.

Visitors who are used to a more hearty breakfast may be pleased to know that many tourist hotels are now providing a full breakfast with choice of eggs, bacon and cold meats and a variety of jams and fruits as well as cereals.

After the workers have breakfasted and begun their daily work the shoppers, usually buying food but increasingly visiting the shops and boutiques which are devoted to fashion and luxury products, appear in the streets. Men too, in a land where the quality and style of one's clothes is a mark of social status, may be seen shopping at the stores in which British male fashions are considered the smartest.

The midday break is often announced in towns by the blast of a factory siren usually at 1 pm. Shops may stay open until 1.30 pm and museums, in deference to their visitors, sometimes do not close until 2 pm but do not open again in the afternoon. Those that do will usually re-open at about 5 pm, staying open until 8 pm.

As work stops so the bars begin to fill with customers who gather to meet friends, drink a glass of wine or a manzanilla, a light sherry type of wine or a dry sherry. To accompany the drinks there are **tapas** which may be simply crisps and olives or prawns, mussels, langoustines or squid rings. Once these appetizers were free and decorated the bar counters in great abundance but now they have to be ordered and paid for, except for the crisps and olives. After the prelunch drinks most Spaniards will head home, causing severe traffic jams, for their lunch, the main meal of the day. In summer this produces a somnolence which can only be alleviated by a siesta so everything stops until about 4.30 pm. For visitors, however, the long afternoon shut down is an exasperation as all museums, art galleries and shops are closed.

At 5 pm, the hour when bullfights start, everyone is back in action, refreshed and full of energy. Shop shutters roll up with a rattle and bang, church doors creak open, street vendors begin their perambulations and the traffic jams begin anew.

At 7 pm or 8 pm the long evening begins with another gathering at the bars for the **tertulia**, literally the conversation, which is the real reason for the gatherings not the drinking itself. Spaniards are gregarious by nature and always eager to talk, which makes them admirable hosts for foreign visitors who take the trouble to learn their language. The pleasant aspect of the tertulia is that it provides entertainment for everyone, rich and poor, young and old, male and female. Not so long ago the tertulia was dominated by adult males while married ladies, spinsters and widows stayed at home in their sober dresses, and the young were not allowed out at all. Now everyone goes out for a pleasant evening's amusement. And what can be more amusing than watching other people? The wives accompany the husbands and bring the young children too, the widows and spinsters put on their best dresses and meet for a jolly gossip over a glass of wine and the young meet at their own bars, usually tiny places where they spill out into the streets quite unaware, it seems, of the motor traffic trying to get by. At about 10.00 pm the move home or to a restaurant begins. The young, who have a curfew agreement with their parents, disperse and the evening becomes tranquil except for those headed for later evening entertainments.

In summer there is still plenty of movement in the streets until well past two o'clock in the morning and it is surprisingly peaceful. There are no bands of drunks, and people walk about the narrow streets of the old parts of the towns and cities without apparent anxiety despite the absence of armed police who once were conspicuous in Franco's Spain. This does not apply, however, to the Costas of Spain where crime is on the increase and the piropo (compliment) which Spanish men once addressed to women in the streets has become more like an insult.

The fiestas

The Spanish, though on the whole a reserved and hard working people, enjoy their fiestas many of which have religious origins. Many of these fiestas are still authentically regional and have not become merely a tourist attraction like so many once genuine expressions of local beliefs and feelings in other countries. It is therefore well worth making an effort to attend a fair or festival that may be taking place during your visit to Spain.

The first national celebration of the year is **Carnival** which although pagan in origin is firmly attached to the idea of enjoying oneself before Lent imposes abstention from certain kinds of food and other pleasures. Carnival embodies the idea of permissiveness which, in the Galician festival in particular, includes behaviour which in normal times would be considered anti-social such as throwing flour or coloured powder and water over other participants in the celebration. The main element of Carnival is the processions of floats, fancy dress and in particular the wearing of masks to disguise the true identity of the individual. In many towns in Spain the end of Carnival is still marked by the burning of the Carnival king, a sign that the period of permissiveness is over. Among the most celebrated Carnival celebrations are those of **Cadiz** which is marked by processions, carnival floats, choirs and dancing, **Bielsa** near Huesca and **Lanz** in Navarre where a giant Carnival king is the centre of the festival.

The Lent period is ended by **Holy Week,** which is also celebrated throughout Spain with outstanding ceremonies at

Baeza, Arcos de la Frontera, and Bercianos de Aliste (Zamora) and particularly in Seville, the most famous of all Holy Week celebrations. Here on every day between Palm Sunday to the eve of Easter Sunday there are processions from various churches to the cathedral. These feature floats, carried by men, or sometimes on wheels and are accompanied by the hooded figures of members of the various religious fraternities. The gilded candelabra, the tortured figures of Christ crucified, the resplendent robes of madonnas and saints, lit by candles and torches make a strange and moving spectacle even for sceptics, though there are few of these in the vast crowds that follow the processions.

Holy Week is followed by the **Seville Fair** an extraordinary outburst of colourful celebrations, there are processions of carriages and horses, with riders and passengers dressed in traditional Sevillian costumes, there are gipsies, stalls where flamenco is performed throughout the evenings, bullfights and illuminations and non-stop entertainment. Although the fair is now a famous tourist attraction it is still firmly attached to the religious roots from which the celebration sprang.

A very different kind of spring fair is the **Fallas of Valencia** when the city, which is the centre of the immensely productive fruit and vegetable farms of the region, celebrates St Joseph's Day. St Joseph was a carpenter and the large scale conflagrations which are a feature of the Valencia festival are symbolic of the burning of wood shavings by the brotherhood of Valencian carpenters in the Middle Ages. Today the bonfires are more ambitious and huge edifices are built only to be burned down amid fireworks, music, dancing and much eating and drinking by everyone, except the fire brigade who are on emergency standby through the festival.

A historical theme runs through some of the other festivals of the beginning of the year. In January **Granada** celebrates the taking of the city by the Catholic Monarchs with colourful pageantry. A more warlike celebration of the defeat of the Moors takes place later in the Spring on St George's Day at Alcoy, near Alicante. This festival named **Moros y Christianos** re-enacts the battles between Moors and Christians with members of the population dressed for the part. The three day celebration includes music and dancing and concludes with an attack on a mock castle with victory for the Christians, though they are usually outnumbered by the Moors whose picturesque costumes attract more volunteers.

Many people are not aware that at Jerez de la Frontera horses and horsemanship are as much part of local tradition as sherry. This equine connection is celebrated at an important **Jerez Horse Fair** in early spring when, as well as the usual events of a horse show, there are several days of Andalucian entertainment including flamenco. Though less well known than the Seville Fair the festival of Jerez de la Frontera is considered by many to rival it in colour and quality.

In May, the month when the hot sun of Andalucía is bringing out the summer flowers, there is an unusual festival in Cordoba. The **Festival of the Patios** is based on the decoration and flowering of the many colonnaded patios inside the houses of the city as well as the streets. The blaze of colour that invades the city streets sets the mood for a week of celebration and entertainment including bullfights.

The most famous festival of bullfight, thanks to Ernest Hemingway who wrote about in it *'The Sun Also Rises'*, is the one at Pamplona in Navarre which takes place in July at the feast of St Firminus or **San Fermin**. Though the festival has become the world's most attended celebration of bullfighting something of its original flavour remains at the Encierro of the bulls, that is the running of the bulls from their pens to the bullring. This provides an occasion for all those who feel it necessary to demonstrate their macho qualities by running in front of the bulls or even just by being in the street in one of the doorways, as James Michener describes in his voluminous tome **Iberia.** Those who do not feel the need to prove themselves hang out of windows watching the spectacle which despite its reputation rarely proves fatal to anyone. If you wish to join in the fun with greater safety go to the bullring and try your skill against a calf with padded horns which is released after the bulls have been locked away.

When the bulls are not running or being despatched in the bullring the visiting population which is greater than the resident one, amuses itself by getting drunk or attending the various flamenco and other kinds of entertainments which make up this world famous event.

July is also the month of one of the great religious festivals of Spain – that of **Santiago de Compostela**. Though there are still all year round pilgrims to the shrine of the patron saint of travellers and ally of the Christians against the Moors, the second half of July is the peak season for visitors to the cathedral city. During this time processions, dancing displays, and firework shows entertain the visitors whose numerous embraces of the mint's bronze statue have given him an added lustre.

A traditional festival which has continued unchanged in Spain and has not become a tourist attraction is the **Romería**, a pilgrimage on horseback or on horse drawn vehicle to the shrine of a saint. This is a rather grand and colourful kind of picnic rather like the trip to the waterfall described by Laurie Lee in his *A Rose in Winter*. A great deal of food and wine is consumed, guitars are played, singers burst into song, dancers dance and everyone enjoys themselves. One of the best attended Romerías of Andalucía is the one to the Sanctuary of Our Lady of El Rocio (**Nuestra Señora del Rocio**) which attracts gipsies from the Seville area as well as from the port of Huelva. This takes place at Whitsun. There are other Romerías throughout the summer months throughout Spain which are well worth seeing.

In Catalonia festivals usually involve the building of Castellers or human pyramids at which Catalans excel. Among these are the September festival of Our Lady of Mercy (**Nuestra Señora de la Merced**) celebrated in Barcelona. This is an occasion for general festivities with the two activities which have become symbols of Catalonian independence; the dancing of the Catalan Sardana in the streets and squares of the city and the human pyramid building which reaches quite astonishing heights and keeps the spectators keyed up with suspense.

The charm of all Spanish fiestas is their unspoilt, unsophisticated character. They lack the smoothly orchestrated organisation of the spectacular public entertainments engineered for public relations or tourist purposes in other countries. In Spain festivals are essentially by, with and for the people themselves. You can enjoy them not merely as a spectator of a procession of floats or a gigantic firework display but as one of a community sharing a common pleasure in bars, in the streets and squares, in restaurants.

A typical item of most Spanish festivals which seems to embody the spirit of the fiesta is the appearance of the giants and big heads (**Gigantones and Cabezudos**) which roam about the streets. These figures contain perspiring stalwarts who propel them about and release all kinds of emotions from the crowds – awe, fear, amazement, ribaldry, impudence. As they march about to the sound of a local band (bagpipes and drums in northern Spain) the children run among them pushing and slapping the figures who retaliate by hitting at their attackers with pigs bladders attached to a string on a stick; a game that evokes medieval times. Meanwhile, the adult spectators call out warnings or console the unfortunates who have received an unexpected blow.

Among the figures there are familiar faces; Ferdinand and Isabella are among the historic celebrities but others bear a surprising resemblance to other well known faces – Juan Carlos, Princess Diana, President Reagan – or is it merely coincidence?

When the fiesta is over the gigantones and cabezudos, the holy effigies and other creatures of the festival return to their abodes in churches and barns. If you see them there you cannot help feeling that they are live beings asleep until the spirit of Spanish fiestas makes them come alive again.

Shopping

At one time most travellers in Spain returned home with a straw hat or basket, a pair of castanets or tambourine decorated with a picture of a bullfight, a ceramic tile and a few litres of wine. Fashions change, however, except in wine, and the souvenirs that were once 'de rigeur' are getting more difficult to find.

28

Some of the traditional souvenirs have taken a new lease of life however. The objects of straw are more likely to be plain instead of decorated with bright coloured raffia. The ceramics are increasingly plain, glazed or handpainted by contemporary potters with modern versions of old designs. Some of these are extremely fine but the price is higher than it once was.

In the cities, shops are acquiring a boutique look with the goods arranged in the style familiar in most European cities. Often the goods are expensive, more than one would expect in a country where the average standard of living is still low compared to the more advanced industrial countries. Moreover there are a great many imported products. The sad fact is, as one unperturbed shop assistant told me, there is no point in buying hand made earthenware kitchen pots when one can buy plastic ones at half the price that will last twice as long. Market stalls once loaded with delightfully decorated plates and jugs now sell plastic buckets and aluminium pans, and the rolls of lace are more likely to come from Taiwan than some hard pressed village in Castile.

There are, however, many things to tempt the visitor but they are not cheap. Spanish leather is still a good buy, and ladies shoes and handbags well designed and carefully finished. Embroidered lingerie and blouses are still luxuriously made and a joy for a goodly length of time. Mantillas, even if you do not feel you can wear one are still beautifully embroidered by hand and Toledo knives and damascene work are still made by craftsmen.

Travellers for whom shopping for clothes is part of a holiday may be a little disappointed however to find themselves looking at window displays full of the products of Burberry and Jaeger and to hear that Marks and Spencer are setting up shop in Spanish department stores.

In the event that you are tempted, however, we add the following table of measures.

Shoes

	British	6	7	8	9	10
Men's	European	40	41	42	43	44
	USA	6½	7½	8½	9½	10½

Shoes (cont)

		4	5	6	7	8
Women's	British	4	5	6	7	8
	European	36	37	38	39	40
	USA	5½	6½	7½	8½	9½

Dresses

British	10/32	12/34	14/36	16/38	18/40
European	38	40	42	44	46
USA	8	10	12	14	16

Men's Collar Sizes

British/USA	14	14½	15	15½	16	16½	17
European	36	37	38	39	41	42	43

Weight

	(¼ kg)			(½ kg)		(¾ kg)		(1 kg)	
grams	50 100 150 200 250 300	400	500	600	700 750 800 900 1000
ounces	0 1 2 3 4 6 8 12	16	·	24	32	36
	(¼ lb) (½ lb)	(1 lb)	(1½ lb)	(2 lb)	(2¼ lb)

☆ ☆ ☆ ☆ ☆

La Corrida de Toros

For spectators the core of the corrida's attraction lies, as in most dangerous sports, in the possibility that someone will get hurt or killed. This is what keeps everyone on the edge of their seats munching peanuts and taking swigs out of the quarter size bottles of brandy sold by the ringside vendors.

Most bullfighters know this whether they are matadors (the ones who will despatch two out of the six bulls of the corrida), banderilleros (the ones who will place the decorated darts on the bulls' back) or picadors (who ride horses and plunge their lances into the bulls' neck muscles). Bullfighters who want to make their name, or those who are fading, therefore do everything they can to amaze the spectators. For example, they kneel before the bull and put their elbow on its forehead and their hand to their ears as if telephoning (for this reason this manoeuvre is called 'el telefono') or they stand with their backs to the bull and stretch out their arms to the crowd defying fate.

Though matadors who are at the top rarely go in for such hazardous tricks these routines are a part of the bullfight which is in fact a kind of theatre. The dramatic structure was given to the Corrida by Francisco Romero who was born in Ronda in 1698.

Before Romero the bullfight was a fight in which high born gentlemen pitted their own skill and their horses agility against wild bulls armed only with a lance. In fact, it was a typically medieval activity designed to show the physical courage and prowess of those who ruled the land. This sport still lives on today among the rich who can afford to risk a string of beautiful thoroughbred horses in this exciting, beautiful and deadly encounter.

Romero turned the sport into the popular dramatic entertainment, with a prologue and three acts, that you see today. The prologue consists in the presentation of the cast of 'matadors' in their splendid embroidered suits of Light, (three for each corrida) 'banderilleros' (three for each matador) and picadors (one for each matador's two bulls) followed by various assistants like the 'monosabios' (wise monkeys) who hold the pica-dors horse and the 'mulilleros' who drag the dead bull off with their team of mules.

Accompanying the actors is the 'alguacil' (mounted official) in sombre 16th century costume and cape who receives the key thrown down from the box of the President of the corrida as a signal to the start the action. While all this is going on a band in which brass instruments predominate plays traditional corrida tunes, often paso dobles dedicated to famous matadors.

The door of the bull pen now opens and a bull rushes into the arena through the gate known as the toril. Occasionally it will walk in looking bewildered in which case it will be booed and hissed and if it continues to act in a cowardly fashion will receive insults and cushions and other missiles. If these fail to rouse the animal then the President of the Corrida orders the creature off to be made into chops and steaks without the honour and glory that will come to the other, braver bulls.

The bull is then enticed round the area by bullfighters who wave large coloured capes while the matador looks on and assesses the bull's fighting style, the manner and direction in which it hooks and its way of running, stopping, turning etc. The trumpet now sounds and a more sombre act begins with the picadors, who are generally large men in a kind of Sancho Panza costume, mounted on horses that appear to have escaped from a knacker's yard. The bulls are now encouraged to charge the horses and receive a thrust from the lance which penetrates the muscles in their neck making a large hole through which blood begins to spout. The picador is allowed three pics by which time he should have done enough damage to the bull to weaken its neck muscles. In these encounters the horses are also damaged by the sheer impact of a ton or so of bull, and by the horns, though as the horses side is covered with a mattress this unpleasantness is not visible.

The redeeming feature of the second act is the work of the matadors in drawing the bull away from the horse when it gets knocked over or is in some other hazardous situation. The 'quite' or taking way is accompanied by some fine cape work with beautiful and elegant passes known by various names such as 'veronica', when the cape is drawn over the bulls head, the 'molinete', when the matador spins round making a colourful whirlpool, the 'delantal', where the cape is spread out before the matador like an apron.

A trumpet announces the end of the picadors performance and the third act begins. This is carried out by the banderilleros who invite the bull to charge and then run nimbly across his line of movement placing two decorated darts in the wound in his back. Sometimes the matador will perform this act and very foolhardy ones will even snap the banderillas in half thus reducing their distance from the bull as the banderillas are placed.

The fourth and final act is the faena – or opus – of the matador who appears now with a short cape (muleta) and sword and salutes the President of the Corrida and occasionally dedicates the bull he is about to kill to a ringside celebrity. The matador now has to reduce the bull to a state of immobility which will allow him to plunge the sword into the spot where it will penetrate to the heart. In the course of his faena he performs various passes such as 'derechazo' in which he extends the muleta with his right hand, 'de pecho' which brings the bulls head up past the matadors chest etc.

Having reduced the bull to a standstill the matador now lines up for the kill, sighting down the sword for the spot where it must enter the bull for a clean kill. The final thrust can be the result of the matador moving in on the bull 'a volapie' or inciting the bull to run towards the matador 'recibiendo'. If the job is well done the matador is cheered, 'ole's' echo round the arena and the matador may be given one or two of the bull's ears or even its tail in recognition of his performance. More often than not the sword goes in crooked and hits the bulls lungs so that it chokes to death in its own blood, or hits a bone and sticks halfway. After several failed attempts the matador uses the 'estoque', a sword with a cross piece, with which he attempts to penetrate the base of the bull's brain. When this fails but the bull has sunk to the floor it is despatched with a dagger thrust into the brain.

Whether you approve of it or not there is no doubt

33

that a Corrida makes the adrenalin flow more than any other spectator sport and there is also no doubt that its artistic presentation obscures objective moral judgement. It is also certain that it will be a long time, if ever, before the Corrida disappears from the Spanish scene. To think that football will replace it is a dream; on the other hand, I must admit that there are more good football matches than good corridas. But football will never provide the intense and absorbing spectacle of death in the afternoon.

Note: Bullfight seats are sold at special booths situated in central parts of the town. Hotel concierges can also get them for you. Seats are broadly speaking divided between those in the sun (sol) and those in the shadow (sombra) and the ones nearest the ringside are the most expensive. Seating is on concrete tiers and cushions are sold at the entrace to the arena.

☆ ☆ ☆ ☆ ☆

Motoring in Spain

Spain is a large country (the third largest in Europe) of some 581,000 km^2 (224,325 sq miles) and its town and cities are often far apart with little habitation between them. Railways and air services are good but networks are limited. Bus services are more expensive but even they do not cover the small villages or isolated castles that make travelling in Spain memorable. The only way to see Spain properly is therefore by car, either a hired one or your own.

• Roads

Roads in Spain vary considerably in quality. The best surfaced, fastest and most dangerous are the motorways (autopistas), but there are few of these. The main motorways being the one that goes round the Mediterranean coast, the one from Irun to Bilbao, and the one from Bilbao to Barcelona. The others are short stretches from Seville to Cadiz and around Madrid.

Most main roads are national routes (carretera nacional). These are metalled roads but often lack road markings and well maintained shoulders. Often the shoulders are below

34

the metalled road level or full of potholes. Regional roads (carreteras comarcales) can have anything from metalled to gravel surfaces and are often narrow. Signposting is not abundant and it is wise to carry a good map, specially if you are travelling off a main road.

A great effort is being made to improve the standard of Spanish roads and you may come across miles of roads that are being surfaced or re-made.

● Traffic

In Spain everyone drives on the right, or is supposed to but where there are poor road surfaces most people drive where the road looks best. On the whole this means that cars are usually driven along the middle of the road. In towns the traffic congestion also impels impatient motorists to occupy the lane of oncoming traffic. Watch out at corners.

Most Spanish cities are old and many ingenious and incomprehensible (to visitors) one way systems have been devised to ease the congestion. Some writers have suggested that this is so bad that either you hire a taxi driver to guide you to your destination or park the car, once there, and walk or take taxis. Personally I have not found the Spanish cities any worse than say Paris or Rome. With sufficient patience and alertness everything comes out allright in the end.

On the open road there is usually little traffic unless you are on a road used by a large articulated lorries. Usually lorry drivers will signal with their rear lights when the road is clear (port or left hand indicator) and when not (starboard or right hand indicator). Some impatient motorists try to overtake on corners and blind spots on the road. Therefore, when approaching a line of traffic behind a lorry, and when you are on a blind corner or hill slope you should remember there may be a lorry and car queue out of sight.

● Petrol

Petrol stations are few and far between so you should never allow the petrol gauge to fall below one quarter full. Petrol (super or regular) is usually bought by money amounts, and many service stations take credit cards. It is usual to tip when receiving extra service, about 30 to 50 pesetas is ample.

35

• Speed restrictions

Speed limits in Spain are 120 km (77 mph) on motorways, 100 km (60 mph) on other roads, 40 km (25 mph) in built up areas. Needless to say most people ignore these limits but if you get caught you will receive a ticket and a fine. There are few police about in the countryside and town traffic police are usually so busy blowing whistles and directing traffic that they rarely have time for more than excited expostulations to the erring driver. In Spain as in most countries people who are normally courteous and polite become transformed from el Doctor Jekyll to el Sēnor Hyde when behind the wheel of a car.

Even so Spain is a wonderful country to drive through though some people accustomed to the endless procession of small villages and river valleys, hills and dales or other European countries find at first that the vast expanses of meseta or the rolling olive covered hills of Andalucía are boring. It is all a question of mental attitude. In Spain a car journey is like a voyage in a small boat across an open sea where every now and again you come across an island, a promontory or some people. The sense of discovery is constantly there and the rewards are many.

Glossary

• Architectural

Alcazaba – a fortified building within a town, often with a barracks.

Alcázar – a royal Moorish palace, also fortified at times.

Artesonado – a coffered ceiling, often with star shaped panels.

Azulejos – glazed ceramic tiles.

Baroque – a highly ornate style of architecture with large, rounded sculptural forms.

Churriguresque – an extreme kind of baroque invented by the Churriguera family.

Gothic – a style of architecture based on arches and buttresses to support the weight of a building. This allowed greater window space than was possible in Romanesque architecture. Spanish Gothic did not develop into the elegant perpendicular style of Northern Europe as exemplified by Chartres or Salisbury cathedrals.

Isabelline – a very decorative style of stone work developed at the time of Ferdinand and Isabella which was more like applied decoration than a structural style such as Baroque.

Mudéjar – a name for architecture by Moors who lived in Christian dominated territories. Only distinguishable from Moorish work by an expert.

Plateresque – a decorative Renaissance style of architecture which evokes the characteristics of the work of silversmiths.

Romanesque – an early medieval style based on solid walls to hold up the roof, with small window spaces and rounded arches.

● **Places**

Bodega – a wine producer's store or cellar.

Bodegón – a wine cellar/bar that serves snacks or food.

Fonda – a very cheap pension.

Hostal – a simple inn, although also used for upmarket hotels that cultivate an old inn atmosphere eg Hostal de la Gavina.

Lonja – a building used for an exchange-wool, stock market etc.

Marisqueria – a seafood restaurant.

Mercado – market.

Palacio – a noble mansion.

Plaza de Toros – bullring.

Taifa – name for the disunited small kingdom of the Moors.

Notes

● **Names**

The names of places, buildings and the points of interest are printed in bold type. On the whole we have given the English version first followed by the Spanish in brackets. In the Basque country, Catalonia, we have given the Spanish name using the Basque and Catalan as well where they are totally different. Smaller, less interesting places have been left in standard type to avoid a profusion of bold names.

• Hotels

Hotels mentioned in the text are top quality hotels and paradors because after a hard day's drive and sightseeing it is worth rewarding yourself with a bit of luxury. Prices of all the hotels except for those in Madrid, Barcelona, Seville are around £25 per night. The great hotels of Madrid, Barcelona, San Sebastian and Seville are double that. All hotels in Spain are kept up to high standards in the category and you cannot go far wrong by using the hotels list provided by the Spanish Tourist office or in the Red Michelin guide.

• Restaurants

We have included very few restaurants in this book because apart from the top rate ones which aim at cuisine rather than plain cooking, there is a vast choice and it comes down to personal preference and taste. Personally I like to window shop for every meal, strolling around restaurant areas, looking at the menus shown outside, peering in to see if the restaurant has the right kind of atmosphere. If you need guidance look in the Red Michelin.

• Motoring itineraries

These have been provided to give you some ideas on how to enjoy the region to the full, without over-taxing yourself by lengthy arduous journeys. The itinerary includes suggestions for accommodation, and where practical paradors have been recommended. The routes are for guidance only and you should double check the state of the roads with the local tourist office or hotel manager.

Chapter Two:
The gateway to Mediterranean Spain

The first wave of the tourist invasion that has transformed the coasts of Spain in less than half a century broke on the coast of Catalonia in the 1950s. The visitors came largely from Britain as other parts of Europe had not recovered from the effects of World War II. There were a few Belgians and Dutch, some Scandinavians, not many French, for they had not yet discovered that other countries could be as attractive as their own, and no Germans or their allies.

Of course, there had been holiday travellers in Spain long before the 20th century but they had been few. Francis Bacon had travelled in Spain in 1629 just a few years after the impetuous visit of Prince Charles, James I's son, in pursuit of a marriage with a Spanish Infanta. It was Bacon who wrote the aphorism that would later apply to the British Empire: 'the sun never sets in the Spanish Dominions, but ever shines on one part or another of them.' Even in the 19th century, Spain was not an easy country. The inveterate traveller, Augustus Hare, travelling in Spain in 1873, commented 'he who would really see Spain, must go prepared to rough it,' adding 'it is also necessary at once to lay aside all false expectations.'

Forcing the gates of Franco's Spain

Most people who went to Spain in the 1950s had no expectations, for Spain was an unknown country, isolated from the world by the revolutions of the 1920s, the civil war of 1936-39, and the world war against the Nazis and fascists who had helped Franco to establish his dictatorship. The

1950s' tourists were the first to arrive en masse in Spain, most of them travelling by train to Port Bou at the eastern end of the frontier with France. Here, they had to change trains because Spanish railways ran on a different gauge and undergo the emigration and customs formalities of a country which had seen few European holidaymakers in recent years and never so many at the same time. The tourists would be ushered into a large corrugated-iron shed which, in summer, became hot enough to serve as an oven for cooking the traditional Catalonian (Catalunyan) hotpot Fabas a la Catalana. Once the trainload was inside all doors were closed and the citizens of a new democratic and socialist Britain faced the representatives of a dictatorship. Among these the most ominous were the Guardia Civil with their guns, patent leather hats and solemn faces.

Neither side knew quite how to comport themselves in this novel confrontation. The Spaniards were loth to lose their dignity and authority by smiling and the travellers were uncertain about the extent of familiarity they could allow themselves. Passports were examined carefully and covered with rubber stamp marks, and luggage was searched for seditious literature, foreign cigarettes or packets of coffee. After the anxious encounter, the doors of the custom shed would be opened and the travellers flowed out onto the Spanish railway platforms. Here wooden carriages as broad as a duenna's posterior awaited them, set comfortably behind large engines which steamed and puffed out clouds of black soot. From the windows of the restaurant car floated the pungent smell of olive oil and garlic, heightening the travellers' awareness that they had arrived in a country quite unlike their own.

Catalonia (Catalunya) the great

It was appropriate that these pioneers of package tourism in Spain should have entered the country through Catalonia, for this north-eastern port of Spain has always been orientated towards the Mediterranean and European cultures. Early traders from the eastern Mediterranean visited its shores, and its ports, whose ruins still survive, were built,

Later, the Romans sent fleets and armies, creating cities, building aqueducts, bridges and roads, and settling their retired legionaries in the land. In the Middle Ages Catalonia, politically linked with Aragon and with territory stretching as far down the eastern coast as Valencia, dominated the western Mediterranean and had colonies on the Balearics, in Sicily, Malta and in mainland Greece.

The Catalonian alliance with Aragon was not entirely beneficial. While the Catalans were absorbed in maintaining their sea trade against the Genoese, the Aragonese, though profiting from the maritime success of their allies, were dallying with the new power of Castile. Situated in Central Spain, the Castilians had been building up alliances with the powers of Northern Europe. Among these was England, with whom dynastic links were forged: Eleanor, the daughter of Ferdinand III of Castile, married Edward I and, a century later, the daughters of Castilian King Pedro the Cruel married John of Gaunt and Edmund Langley, brothers of the Black Prince. These latter unions had a strange and romantic outcome. Pedro the Cruel, who had asked for the Black Prince's help when he had been driven from his throne, was assassinated some years later by the illegitimate Henry II of Castile. To avenge the murder and, no doubt, to claim the throne for his wife, Constance of Castile, John of Gaunt, Duke of Lancaster, invaded Castile. However, once there instead of waging war he came to an amicable arrangement by which his daughter, Catherine of Lancaster, became the wife of Henry III of Castile.

The strengthening of Aragon and Castile by these foreign marriages left Catalonia out of the mainstream of Spanish affairs. Then disasters in its maritime trade and financial difficulties, as well as the plague that raged throughout Europe in the 14th century, enfeebled the once proud nation. Matters grew worse when Aragon and Castile were unified with the marriage of Ferdinand of Aragon and Isabel of Castile in 1474.

The reign of these two monarchs whose mission in life was to unite Spain as a single Catholic country was disastrous for Catalonia. The discovery of America in 1492 began a shift in the centre of trade from Spain's Mediterranean coast to the Atlantic, though the full effect of this would not be felt for a hundred years. A more immediate cause for alarm was the persecution of Jews and Moors which the Catholic monarchs set in motion.

Though the Arab invaders of Spain had been in retreat since the defeat of their armies by Charles Martel in the 8th century, the Moorish people who settled in Spain had continued to live on unmolested. In Catalonia they were appreciated for their contribution to science, the arts and for their craftmanship. Similarly the Jews were a part of the community and contributed to its commercial welfare.

The campaign of the Catholic monarchs against all non-Catholics drove the Jews and Moors into exile and thus impoverished the life of the nation, which gradually became just another province of Spain which was ruled by Castile.

Catalonian rebirth

The Catalan identity remained submerged throughout the Golden Age of Spain in the 16th and 17th centuries. The Catalans made one desperate effort to escape from the clutches of the central government by siding with the English and Dutch in the War of the Spanish Succession. Unfortunately, the French-Castilian alliance candidate gained the Spanish throne through the Treaty of Utrecht and once again Catalonia found itself on the losing side. The territory was reconquered by Philip V, the new Bourbon King, in 1714.

A revival of Catalan fortunes came about in the 19th century when the liberal movements that were sweeping across Europe created an opportunity for submerged cultural groups to re-assert themselves. In France, Frederic Mistral had started a Renaissance of the Provincial culture and in Catalonia the poets Jacinto Verdaguer and Juan Madragall led to a movement for Catalan freedom.

The reborn Catalonia had all the hallmarks of the region's traditional character. The spirit of independence that had created a great maritime trading power and the stubborn individualism that had made them ungovernable rose again

GATEWAY TO MEDITERRANEAN SPAIN

in the extreme forms, perhaps as a result of their long suppression.

In the 1830s there was a wave of anti-establishment rioting with the burning of churches and expulsion of the priests who had for so long been an arm of government. By the 1920s the Catalan Anarchist movement, whose followers rejected any control of political life by central governments, was the most avant-garde in Europe. When King Alfonso XIII abdicated in 1931 in response to the general dissatisfaction throughout Catalonia and most of Spain, Catalonia declared itself a republic.

The region's freedom was shortlived. In 1936 General Franco and his army made their bid to take over the government and unite Spain politically. The coup failed and Spain was plunged into a Civil War in which half a million people were killed. During the war first Valencia then Catalonia became the headquarters of the Republican forces. When these were finally overcome, in 1939, Catalonia once more suffered a severe repression of its national culture. With the defeat of Franco's World War II European fascist allies and a loan from the United States the regime began to adopt a more tolerant attitude and to open its frontiers to visitors from other countries.

Catalonia today

Thus Spain and Catalonia began a new life, one which with Franco's death took on the most promising prospects since Spain's Golden Age. Under the new young King, Juan Carlos, the attempts to eradicate the national cultures of the Spanish regions were forgotten and a more tolerant attitude began to prevail. In Catalonia this had brought about a revival of both the national language, which is now seen on signposts and in shops, and of its national culture. It has also brought about a liberation of the enterprise spirit which has made Catalonia one of the most flourishing regions of Spain. In the 1950s Catalonia led the way in developing the tourism industry which now provides much needed national revenue, and today it is a leader in manufacturing and commerce.

43

There has been a price to pay. The once almost deserted coastline of the Costa Brava, one of the most beautiful in Europe, has been densely urbanised wherever the rugged nature of the land allows. In addition Catalonia's success has attracted scores of thousands of the impoverished and jobless people of Andalucia. Expansion has therefore brought its problems but much of what is beautiful and true in Catalonia remains, especially in the interior, and the people are still as vital, hospitable, and hardworking as they ever were. As an admirer, one can only reflect on the truth of what Charles V, the most powerful ruler of Europe and the Americas, said in 1519: 'I would rather be the Count of Barcelona than the King of the Romans.'

Barcelona

If Barcelona is the heart of Catalonia, then the **Ramblas** are the arteries through which pumps the life blood of the city. As boulevards the Ramblas may not be as grand as the Champs Elysées but they have a life quality unsurpassed by any other city avenues. Through them and in them you can get a 24-hour, non-stop spectacle of every aspect of the life of the city and indeed of human nature. The Ramblas are not wide but they have room for a central mall shaded by plane trees and lined with seats; on each side the traffic runs endlessly up one side and down the other. Enclosing the whole narrow and ever-active corridor are houses, most of them built at the turn of century or earlier.

This long boulevard is, in fact, made up of several Ramblas. At the port end, near where Columbus stands on his column at the Plaza Portal de la Pau overlooking a full-scale model of his Santa María, is the Rambla de Santa Monica. In the days of Catalan's supremacy as a maritime power this was the sailors' quarter. The **Royal Arsenals** (twelve of them, christened the '12 apostles') supplied Charles V with armaments for his ships and the bars and brothels provided sailors with the pleasures of which they had been deprived during their months at sea. Though shipping has much declined in recent years, the bars are less fashionable than in other parts of the Ramblas, the Rambla de Santa Monica still has a salty air about it and there is a fine Maritime Museum in what were once the Royal Arsenals (Rieales Ataranzas).

The real centre of Ramblas' life starts at the Plaza del Teatro, a small square which marks the beginning of the Rambla de los Capuchinos. Here the bars proliferate, usually crowded with students, tourists and prostitutes, the last-named sometimes hardly distinguishable from the rest of the female clientele but at others outrageously flamboyant. Prostitution is an acceptable and longstanding business in Barcelona and not even Franco attempted to stamp it out, though the anarchists of the '20s and '30s used to paste up posters exhorting the girls to give up their demeaning careers. This part of the Ramblas like the Plaza Real is also the gay quarter of Barcelona and after 10 pm you can be witness here to one of the most exotic aspects of city life. If you have a taste for the mysteries of the night you only have to walk fifty yards down one of the side streets to the left to find yourself in the red light district of the Barrio Chino, the "chinese quarter", though no Chinese are visible in its dark streets.

The Rambla de los Capuchinos was once the centre of the Barcelona theatre district, where theatre-goers elegant in evening dress would stroll under the plane trees. Today, it is the main meeting place of all Barcelona. In the early morning it is busy with people going to work or having a coffee at the tables of one of the many cafés. Sweepers are cleaning up the debris of the previous night's crowds and those who have spent the night on the uncomfortable wooden chairs are having their shoes shined as they read the news in La Vanguardia.

From mid-morning the Rambla de los Capuchinos is a scene of restless activity centred on the Rambla San José where the Barcelona market has a wonderful array of vegetables, fruit and fish, so fresh and brilliant in colour that you do not need a painter's eye to feel an instant exhilaration at just looking at them. On the central mall of the Rambla the flower sellers are out in force, their exuberant blooms protected by simple awnings from the sun and from the bird droppings which are one of the minor hazards of the Ramblas. The exotic atmosphere extends further along the Rambla de los Estudios where mini skyscrapers of caged birds wait to be bought by the citizens of Barcelona, who seem to like having live animals and fish around their homes. After shopping, most people find time to meet friends at the cafés. If you want a treat try the Café de la Opera, a rather plush and fashionable place, situated next to the Liceo opera house itself. Even if you are not going to the opera you should visit the building and see its sumptuous turn of the century interior.

At their northern end the Ramblas lead through the Rambla Canaletes into the Plaza de Cataluña which lies like a vast no-man's land between old Barcelona and the grid-patterned modern metropolis to the north.

The most lively and exciting time of day to be on the great boulevard of the Ramblas is in the evening. At night it seems that the whole of Barcelona gathers there to stroll along the central mall under the plane trees, where what sounds like Barcelona's entire bird population chorus their evensong before settling down for the night. The bars are crowded with people enjoying the tapas (snacks) which are the long-drawn-out prelude to the evening meal proper, which most Spaniards eat between 10 o'clock and midnight. The crowds are particularly dense in the Rambla de los Capuchinos and the Plaza Real, an arcaded square of the Rambla which has the air of an aged stage set. One of the most popular restaurants in the area is **Los Caracoles**, a small picturesque place on a corner with chickens roasting on streetside grills and fish soups served in earthenware dishes. Despite being packed with tourists, it seems to be keeping its character. A better one, though quiet and unpretentious, is **Casa Amaya** further down the Ramblas. After dinner the crowds return for a post-prandial stroll or a coffee and Fundador or one of the many other Spanish liqueurs. Spain also produces most of the famous liqueurs, Benedictine, Cointreau, etc. under licence if you prefer one of these. There are always those on the Ramblas who seem to have nothing better to do than to read the newspapers and magazines of every nationality sold at the kiosks or to talk to their friends.

This permanent but constantly changing population encourages traders, who are always on the move, perhaps offering smuggled goods, and, after the bars have finally closed, selling food and drink. The evening is, of course, the time to venture into the Barrio Chino which lies in the V between the Avenida del Parallelo which runs from the Plaza de la Pau, and the Ramblas. This seedy but picturesque quarter is full of small bars and night clubs and has something of the atmosphere of Montmartre before it was commercialised. In other words, it is where the more tawdry but nevertheless fascinating low life of Barcelona goes on.

● The old quarter (Barrio Gótico)

Less seedy but more medieval, with dark narrow streets with overhanging houses and inner courtyards, is the Barrio Gótico. This is an unlikely name for an area which seems to have little in common with what most of us think of as Gothic architecture. The Barrio Gótico lies within a part of Barcelona once enclosed by Roman walls, bits of which can still be seen embedded in old buildings. It is bound by Banys Nous de la Palla, which follows the course of the old walls, and Via Laietana and sits on a low hill, Mons Taber, where the Iberians first founded a city, and where Hannibal's father, Hamilcar Barca, created a Carthaginian colony from which the name Barcelona is derived.

Like most of the old city, the Gothic quarter is always lively and crowded. Shops, bars and restaurants flourish on the ground floors of the old houses and at its centre lies a spectacular cluster of 14th-15th and 16th century buildings around the impressive **Cathedral**. Known colloquially as 'La Seu', the cathedral is dedicated to Sta Eulalia, whose tomb is in the crypt. She is the most celebrated virgin martyr in Spain, a 12-year-old girl who rebuked the Romans at Mérida for their persecution of the Christians, for which act of defiance she was tortured and burnt to death. It was said that when she died a white dove flew out of her mouth and snow of the purest white covered her body. The cathedral, which is one of the finest examples of Catalan Gothic, was a great deal more impressive before the demands of tourism brought about an illumination of its once awesomely gloomy interior. Although, it must be said, the lights allow visitors to appreciate more fully the soaring architecture of the cathedral's 13th and 14th century builders, the wrought-iron grilles and carved tombs as well as the moor's head suspended under the organ which has, alas, given up the ingratiating habit of vomiting sweets on to the Christian children attending church on feast days. The Cathedral cloister, reached through the Porta de Sant Severo, is a particularly charming little haven enjoyed by noisy white geese, placed there in honour of Sta. Eulalia's unsullied virginity, as well as by visitors seeking a moment's cool respite.

More quiet courtyards may be enjoyed in the 15th-century houses alongside the cathedral, including the Archdeacons House (**Casa del Arcediano**) now the city archives the Bishops Palace (**Palacio Episcopal**). The Kings Square (**Plaza del Rey**) was once also a courtyard, part of the palace of the Counts of Barcelona, and has several interesting buildings on its bounds. Among these are the Chapel of **St Agata**, another lady who suffered barbarities at the hands of the Romans, including the cutting off of her breasts; the **Mirador del Rey Martin**, a 15th-century galleried building; and the **Salon de Tinell** where, legend has it, Ferdinand and Isabella received Columbus after his return from America though later they were less favourably disposed to him when the vaunted riches of the Indies did not immediately materialise.

On the western side of the Cathedral from the Plaza del Rey is the Plaza San Jaime and the **Palacio de la Generalidad** the traditional home of the Catalan government since 1539 and the first parliamentary government in Western Europe, and now reinstated after its suspension by Franco. The Generalidad is guarded by a statue of St George, (**San Jorge**) the patron saint of Barcelona. St George, as well as being a slayer of dragons, was also a supporter of the Christian armies of Aragon in their drive to destroy the Moors. He appears several times in the Generalidad building, killing dragons of all shapes and sizes, on foot and on horseback, though not Moors or Jews who were, in fact, treated better in Barcelona than in most Spanish cities. Jews in Barcelona were merely ordered to live in a special quarter, called El Call, to the west of the Plaza de San Jaime, and lived here until 1478 when the Inquisition (and Torquemada) began the persecution of all non-catholics.

Across the square from the Generalidad is the Town Hall (**Ayuntamiento**), which was the headquarters of the Council of 100 which ruled Barcelona from 1372 to 1714 in the style of the Italian city states.

From the Ayuntamiento a narrow alleyway, delightfully named Paradise (**Paradiso**), leads back towards the Cathedral apse past the four corinthian columns which are all the remains of the Roman temple of Augustus. Beyond it is the **Palau del Lloctinent** which houses the archives of the crown of Aragon, a unique collection of medieval documents. Nearby in the **Musco Marés** is the extraordinary collection of statues and ephemera made by the sculptor Frederic Marés. This must be one of the most eccentric collections of objects d'art and bric-à-brac in the world, embodying something of that surrealist spirit which is essentially Catalan and which is evident here in such things as the baby Jesus with real hair, the grinning dancing skeletons and the giant cigars. In them all are the joking, irreverant, surrealist qualities of Gaudi Buñuel, Miró, Dali and Picasso, all of whom were Catalans either by birth or adoption.

● **The deadpan surface**

On the face of it Barcelona is an urbane highly civilised city in which life goes on with dignity and decorum. Along the Paseo de Gracia, which runs north of the Plaza de Cataluña, is the elegant commercial district. Here smartly dressed citizens peer into jewellery shops and fashion boutiques, the urbane international face of money shines brightly. Along the Carrer de Montcada, the 15th-17th century palaces and houses of the hidalgos of the repressive days of Charles V and Philip II suggest a life of tranquility and power.

Appearances are also what the **Plaza d'España** at the foot of the hill of Montjuich is all about, for this architectural show place was set up specially for the Barcelona Exhibition of 1929. The view of the buildings is framed by two tall towers between which you can see fountains, illuminated at night, throwing up a huge torrent of sparkling water before the **Palacio Nacional** on the hill of Montjuich. Housed in the Palacio, an example of 1920s traditional grandeur, is one of the finest art collections in Barcelona (**Museo de Arte de Cataluña**). It will teach the visitor more about the Catalan past than any history book. Here you will find altarpieces and other works of art which evoke the age before Spain was united under the Catholic kings and when Raymond Berenguer of Barcelona was ruler of Provence.

Another relic of the 1929 Exhibition is the Spanish village (**Pueblo Español**) a tourist attraction but one with genuine merit. This village, built especially for the Exhibition, contains full-size replicas of buildings from all parts of Spain. Wrought-iron windowed whitewashed houses of Seville rub shoulders with stone and wood mansions of Aragon, and country houses with flowering balconies from Valencia contrast with the dour facades of La Mancha. Traditional crafts are carried on in street-level shops and workrooms. The main plaza has a stage which resounds at various times to the tap of the Andalucian zapateado, the soft shuffle of the Aragon Jota, and, of course, the machine-gun rattle of the castanets.

● The open spaces

Montjuich is a joy for anyone longing for some green peace after the bustle and hustle of the centre of Barcelona. Its gentle slopes rising 700 ft above the city can be reached by stairs from the Plaza d'España, by cable car from Torre San Jaime or Torre San Sebastian, or by a bus service. From the top is a thrilling bird's eye view of Barcelona.

For an even higher viewpoint, which on clear days allows you to see the Pyrenees, there is **Tibidabo**, at the north-western end of the Avenida Diagonal. This combines a sublime panorama with a gaudy funfair and an ugly church in

GATEWAY TO MEDITERRANEAN SPAIN

a typically Catalonian show of grotesquerie. 'Tibi dabo' comes from the Latin phrase describing the temptations the devil offered to Christ on a high place, 'all these things I will give you'. It would not be difficult to resist the temptations of the Tibidabo but it is a curious place, memorable in its strange mixture of the bizarre, the vulgar and the sublime.

A more down-to-earth park is the **Ciudadela** on the east side of Barcelona. The citadel from which the name of the park is derived was built by Philip V in 1715 to quell the rebellious Catalans after their support of the losing candidate in the War of the Spanish Succession. Needless to say, the Catalans tore it down at the first opportunity – though this did not occur until 1869. Soon after, in 1888, a great Universal exhibition was set up in the park, relics of which include the **Arch of Triumph**, a brick building of the so-called 19th-century Modernists School of Barcelona, which is now used as the Museum of Zoology, and the giant greenhouses.

When the people of Barcelona destroyed the old citadel they rededicated the land on which it stood to nature. The area remains a favourite place for Barcelona families who can be seen at weekends strolling among the trees or watching their children sailing boats in the **Cascada**, an artificial lake with a monumental rocky centrepiece. Others will be strolling towards the **Zoo**, one of the best in Spain, and those with older children may be heading for the **Museo de Arte Moderno**, 'modern' meaning in this case mostly Catalan artists of the 19th and 20th century. Another park well worth a visit, especially if you are bewitched by Gaudi's idiosyncratic creations, is the **Parque Guell**. Here Gaudi's creations are purely for enjoyment; there are giant lizards, a Hall of Columns and a museum of Gaudi's furniture.

☆ ☆ ☆ ☆ ☆

The artistic rebels of Catalonia

Artists associated with Catalonia, however fleetingly, all seem to embody the rebellious, anarchistic spirit of the Catalan, none more so than Antonio Gaudi, the architect. Born in 1852, he embraced the Art Nouveau movement and created out of it something truly original; anathema to some but an expression of genius to others. His great patron, Don Eusebio Guell, commissioned him to build many of the Barcelona buildings with which he is identified, including the Palacio Guell and Park. Gaudi's work is not so much revolutionary as totally beyond the conventional world of architecture. His originality belongs less to the science of structures than to the world of ideas. In a way this is like Catalonia itself, a region bubbling with vitality and ideas which are encouraged to germinate and grow first before becoming systemised later.

Gaudi's most important work in Barcelona is the church of the **Holy Family (Sagrada Familia)** a soaring unfinished construction whose four famous spires rise like space rockets from a welter of organic forms. The Sagrada Familia was begun by another architect who planned a conventional neo-gothic church. It became an obsession with the young Gaudi, who spent the rest of his life trying to complete it. Wrestling with making the improbable possible, Gaudi even took to living in a hut on the site and gave up all other work. When he died in 1126, the building was still unfinished but it has an extraordinary life of its own; haunted by the personality of its maker.

If it ever gets finished – and to enable this to happen you may put your contribution to the cost in the box marked 'for the work', 'para la obra' – it will have three main facades dedicated to the birth, passion and glory of Christ, and each facade will have four towers, making twelve in all, one for each apostle. Four towers will symbolise the evangelists and two further towers will represent the Saviour and the Madonna. With its earth-bound natural forms of the lower structure and the clean space rocket towers, the cathedral will be a titanic symbol of all life between earth and heaven.

This 'earth and heaven' mix is also present in the work of Gaudi's fellow Catalan, Juan Miró, who was born in Barcelona in 1893 and studied painting there, in defiance of his father who wanted him to enter the world of commerce. The earthy character of Miro's early paintings, many of them subjects near Montroig where he lived at his family home after a nervous breakdown, turned later into the ethereal arabesques and splashes of colour of his more famous work. The strange amoebic and thread-like creatures that float in the broth of his tinted canvases have a subreal life, as if seen through the lens of a microscope. In them is that probing into the rhythms and forms that lie below reality which seems a common characteristic of the work of Catalan artists.

In 1975 Miró donated some 290 paintings and sculptures and 300 drawings to the City of his birth which erected a special museum **Juan Miró Foundation** (Fundación Miró) designed by Josef Lluis Sert, to house them.

When Miró left Catalonia for Paris he was introduced to Parisian art circles by Pablo Picasso who, though born in Málaga, spent his formative years in Barcelona. A fine collection of the latter's work is exhibited at the **Museo Picasso** in Carrer di Moncada, a 14th-century palace of Berenguer de Aguila, ruler of Barcelona.

Picasso was brought to Barcelona, via La Coruña in Galicia, by his father who, like many men of Andalucía even today, had had to move to another part of Spain to look for work. Jose Ruiz did everything in his power to help his son along his chosen career, establishing him in the Academia La Llonja and even borrowing funds to send him to study in Madrid, a venture that was not a success. Returning to Barcelona, Picasso became a member of a group of young artists named after their meeting place, the Café of the Four Cats (**Los Cuatro Gatos**). With the help of his new friends, Picasso cut the umbilical cord that had hitherto bound him to his family and began to break out into the radical anarchist world of his contemporaries. But the paintings of his Blue Period had a sad nostalgic air about them as if he himself were pining for the lost world of his early youth

Between 1900 and 1904 Picasso made several abortive trips to Paris but found it difficult to make the final break with his family and with Spain, which suggests that in a sense Cataluña had entered into his soul, perhaps to remain there ever after. Certainly his later uncompromising iconoclasm which broke out in the 'Demoiselles d'Avignon', his first cubist picture, the title of which refers to the girls of a Barcelona brothel, is expressive of the anarchial aspects of the Catalan intellectual life of the period.

At about the time Picasso was struggling with his soul another artist who was to embody the surreal qualities of life as seen through Catalan eyes was just learning to walk. This was Salvador Dali, who was born in Figueras, where a museum devised by him now gives amusement and pleasure to thousands of tourists a year.

Though on the face of it the most outrageous of the artists whose roots lie in the soil of Catalonia, Dali's rebellion against convention was more intellectual than grass roots: even his most eccentric paintings are academic in technique. Nevertheless, he belongs among the riders of the Apocalypse of the established and hierarchical world of Spain, in the same way as Luis Buñuel, the film maker whose first and perhaps most shocking film, **Un Chien Andalou** was conceived with Dali. Buñuel's anticlericalism is in the spirit of Alejandro Lerroux who in 1901, at the height of anarchist extremism, called on all the young barbarians who were setting out to destroy the petrified political systems of the past to 'tear aside the veils of novices and elevate them to the category of mothers'.

☆ ☆ ☆ ☆ ☆

The Costa Brava

The coast from Barcelona to Blanes can offer one or two fine sections but, on the whole, it is a straggle of old houses running by a railway line beyond which lie some stretches of sandy beach. **Blanes** is the first big resort with a good beach, and, though scenically fine, like **Lloret de Mar**, its next-door neighbour, it is crowded, brash, noisy and has all the glitz of a package holiday resort. If you can forget the crowds in the popular resorts in their various forms of beach fancy dress, the smell of suntan oil, the cafés serving Sangriá and Tiá Mariá, the restaurants offering imitation paella, the hideous concrete holiday alcatrazes, then there is much beauty to enjoy. You can discover a coast of rugged rose-coloured cliffs, on which the pines cling precariously, a limpid sea which throws great mantillas of white lace over dark rocks, and narrow calanques with tiny golden beaches where once there were thatched shelters whose owners cooked you fish straight out of an unpolluted sea. In a bygone era you could have dived and swum among shoals of seabass, John Dorys and seabream, and found among the rocks prawns, lobsters and the occasional octopus which would probably have sprayed you with a jet of its black ink. And there were fishermen, poor as stranded mussels, who would take you out in their boats with the huge lamps at the prow which attracted the fish at night. The fishermen are not poor any more, they have taken to running excursions along the coast, and their children go to school, some even to universities. They wear smart suits and aspire to a Seat 500; they already have television. So the ruination of the Costa Brava has its blessings: of a kind.

At **Tossa de Mar**, especially out of high season when the decibels of flamenco have decreased, you can still catch a glimpse of the stunning charm of this ancient port with its 12th-century castle walls and its fishing boats drawn up on the beach. The old village (Vila Vella) and its narrow streets have been preserved. The new developments and camping sites extend up the valley behind the port, and not along the front which is hemmed in by cliffs. These cliffs, sheer, sharply indented, topped with pines and cork trees, make the drive to **San Feliu de Guixols** a continuous delight. San Feliu itself, though no longer the sheltered port which shipped cork to the wine regions of the Mediterranean, still has some charm. Its wide tree-lined esplanade, Paseo Maritimo, still has fisher folk mending nets and the market near the Mozarabic Porta Ferrada is not there just for the tourists. The beach in the harbour is not wonderful so most people go over the promontory to S'Agaro where the fine old hostel now looks down on a scene reminiscent of a Bank Holiday at

55

Bude. All is not lost, however, for as you travel north, the crowds thin a little and the coast around **Calella de Mar**, **Palafrugell**, **Tamariu**, and **Llafranch** is still lovely. Beyond Bagur, however, it becomes less Brava though there are still treasures in store. **Ampurias**, on the Bay of Rosas, is one, the kind of place that haunts you forever; so it should, for people have lived here for 2500 years, though now it is deserted. The earliest to do so were probably Phoeniceans, coming around 500 BC to set up a trading post, with wine, olives, cork, and perhaps grain being exchanged for the products of the Eastern Mediterranean. The sunburned traders prospered enough to interest both Romans and Carthaginians who were casting their eyes around for new markets and sources of products. Scipio Africanus, the destroyer of Carthage took Ampurias, after Hannibal's elephants had proved useless in his Italian campaigns, and built a Roman town behind the Greek port. The ruins are there still among the shifting sand-dunes and whispering Cypresses. Sitting among them, it is easy to imagine the voices of ancient sailors spinning their unbelievable yarns.

The nearest inhabited places to the ruins of Ampurias are at **Sant Marti de Ampurias**, a run-down little village unimproved by tourism, to the north along the deserted beach, and La Escala an unpretentious village with a couple of no-frills hotels which lies to the south. From **La Escala** it is 20 km (12 miles) inland to the motorway; taking this to the south brings one to the old town of **Gerona**, and what romantics might call the real Catalonia. Gerona is not there for the sea and sun-loving tourists; it has a life of its own which has been going on for centuries. The Arabs lived here, building the Arab baths where you can still get steamed and cooled, and the Jews lived in the El Call under the direct protection of the kings until the persecutions of the 15th century.

Christians contributed the Cathedral, which has the widest nave in the world with a span of 22 metres. The 17th-century Baroque stairway into the cathedral is also worth inspection. The art treasures of the cathedral are now housed in the Treasury and in the Art Museum.

The best thing about Gerona is its evocative atmosphere, created by its narrow streets, like Calle Furça which has a great stone gate, its churches like San Feliu, old houses rising along the River Oñar, and ancient walls, which you can walk by way of the Paseo Arqueológico, and its Plaza del Vi where two giants stand in the courtyard of the Teatro Municipal.

If, from the point where you join the motorway at the L'Escala entry, you turn north you come to Figueras, a town interesting today mainly for its museum dedicated to the work of the man who used to eat dead bats when he was a child. We have been entertained by Salvador Dali for years and here, in the town of his birth, the old wizard is still doing his tricks. His home was at nearby Port Lligat, near Cadaques on the coast, a slightly self-conscious, arty place, it overlooks the bay, and is not yet unbearably overcrowded.

Tarragona and the Costa Dorada

The Roman presence is still pervasive in **Tarragona**, a town which the Romans called Tarraco. Sections of the walls of the Roman town, which overlay older Iberian formations and which were themselves topped by sections added by English troops during the War of the Spanish Succession, can be seen along the Paseo Arqueológico. A Roman tower, the Torre de Scipio; a triumphal arch, the Arco de Bara; and an amphitheatre all lie along the old Via Augusta. In the lower town, below the hill on which the ancient town was built, is a necropolis with Roman Christian tombs. The emperors Hadrian and Trajan, both born in Spain, lived in the Praetorium, popularly called Castello del Pilate because legend has it that Pontius Pilate lived there. The Praetorium's tower now houses the Museo de Historia de Tarragona. After the Romans, the Visigoths made Tarragona their capital, but by the Middle Ages it had lost its importance to Barcelona. It became a sleepy, provincial town which remained almost forgotten by the world at large until the 20th-century demand for holidays and wine restored its fortunes.

As a holiday town, Tarragona has immense charm and real character. Its two Ramblas, the Vella in the upper town and

Nova in the lower town, are the centres of town life. There is a fine view of the beach from the Vella along the old ramparts and of the sea from the Balcon del Mediterraneo, and along the tree-shaded Nova the cafés are always lively until long after midnight. Dominating old Tarragona is the Cathedral which, so far, has not been illuminated with fluorescent light and therefore preserves its sombre mystery. Built between the 12th and 15th centuries the cathedral contains a chapel donated by a guild of tailors, Capilla de Santa María de los Sastres, and a superb 12-century cloister.

Tarragona's beach is sandy and popular but it is not as fashionable as **Sitges** further north along the Costa Dorada. Sitges is a resort with the picture postcard characteristics that were bound to make it an 'in' place. It has a church in biscuit-coloured stone on a promontory dividing the two beaches, an old village with white-washed houses where the streets are carpeted with flowers during Corpus Christi, and where boutiques and restaurants abound, and a brand new resort area stretching along the long sandy beach. This is where the young Barcelona set come, including the gays and nudists who have their own beach, the Playa de los Muertos, at Vilanova to the south.

Not too many years ago bathers walking along the Sitges streets in bathing costumes risked arrest but times have changed. Nevertheless Sitges has a certain avant-garde grand tradition for it was here that the more radical elements of Barcelona intellectual life used to gather at the home of the painter and writer Santiago Rusiñol. His house is now the Cau Ferrat Museum.

Other less popular beaches of the Costa Dorada includes **Castelldefels** to the north of Sitges and **Cunit** to the south; still undeveloped, they have long sandy beaches but few of the amenities that many people have come to take for granted on bathing beaches.

Inland from Tarragona along the A2 motorway to **Lérida** are two important 12th-century monasteries which are worth a visit for anyone interested in history or architecture. Both **Santas Creus** and **Poblet** were built in the time of Raymond Berenguer Count of Barcelona when Catalonia and Provence were closely linked and both celebrate the retreat of the Moors from Catalonia. Catalonia and Aragon became allies as a result of the marriage of Berenguer with Petronella, Queen of Aragon, and Poblet became traditionally the temporary home of kings shuttling between the capitals of Barcelona and Zaragoza. Both places were designed as strong points as well as centres of administration and spiritual life. In each, an outer perimeter wall protected the peasants employed in the abbey grounds and an inner wall surrounded the monastic annexcs; a third wall was the final line of defence for the monastery itself. Poblet contains the Royal Pantheon of the kings of Aragon up to the time when Ferdinand and Isabella united Spain and Santa Creus possesses the royal Catalan tombs.

The roads to the Pyrenees

The Catalan Pyrenees are more accessible than the rest of the chain and morc popular. On their border lies the charismatic **Republic of Andorra** which has managed to survive as an independent state throughout the long tussle between France and Spain for dominance in this part of Europe.

The principal road to the Catalan Pyrenees is the 152 from Barcelona to Puigcerda, a distance of 172 km (106 miles) along a route that becomes steeper and more winding as it penetrates into the mountains. The first town of any interest is **Vich** once inhabited by Iberians then Romans. Most of the Pyrennean towns have some fine Romanesque churches but not Vich which knocked down its cathedral, though it retained the belfry, and replaced it by a neo-Gothic one. Some of the medieval art was preserved in the Museo Episcopal.

A longer but worthwhile route to Vich is via the monastery of **Montserrat**, a pilgrimage and sightseeing destination set on the top of stark limestone pinnacles worthy of Gaudi. There is a road up to the top but I suggest you take the cable car which is not only quicker but provides exciting views of the Montserrat mountainside.

59

The monastery was founded in the 10th century by Benedictines and soon became one of the most powerful in Catalonia attracting into its ranks those who found in the Church a route to political power. One of these was Guiliano della Rovere (1443-1513), better known as Pope Julius II, who was renowned for his military prowess (he once went into battle smiting his enemies with his bishop's crozier), as well as for his patronage of Raphael, Michelangelo and Bramante. When Napoleon invaded Spain the monastery had a bad time. General Suchets soldiers hunted the monks among the limestone pinnacles as if they were mountain goats and sacked the buildings which had to be rebuilt in the 19th century.

The object of veneration in the monastery is the black virgin which, according to legend, was hidden from the Moors and rediscovered in the 10th century when a shrine was built to her on this strange and mysterious mountainside with its pinnacles, gorges and caves. The Madonna was not the only find in this mystical ambience for Parsifal discovered the Holy Grail here, a legend which inspired Ignacio de Loyola the soldier and adventurer who became the founder of the Jesuits. He dedicated his sword to the Madonna and the same legend inspired Richard Wagner to write his opera.

To the north lies **Manresa** where Loyola, after receiving the approval of Pope Paul III for his new order, wrote the spiritual exercises essential to the training of Jesuit priests.

From Manresa two roads lead north towards the Pyrenees both converging on **Ripol** the site of the great monastery of Santa María. Like most of the medieval monasteries this was built in a place where the attacks of marauding bands were less likely to occur. Here in relative peace the monks preserved the tatters of Roman civilisation studying the works of Plutarch and Virgil as well as the treatises of Greek philosophers and scientists, some of whose work had become known in Europe through the Moors. Thus in this building of which portals, walls and the cloister remain of the original monastery, founded by Count Wilfred the Shaggy or Hairy, the light of civilisation was kept burning.

From Ripol the 151 road rises through steep pine-clad valleys to the Col D'Ares (1610 m) (5039 ft) and down into Perpignan (France). The 152 continues north to Puigcerda and the road to Foix and Toulouse. To the west runs the 1313 to the **Seo de Urgel**, another seat of the medieval princes, and Archbishops which has a fine 12th-century cathedral and the gateway to Andorra.

Motoring itinerary

Day 1   Barcelona

Sitges	40 k	25 m
Tarragona	51 k	32 m
Poblet	45 k	28 m
Lérida -	48 k	30 m
Total	184 k	115 m

The C 246 goes along the coast from Barcelona to Sitges and beyond the resort to Vendrell where you take the N340 to Tarragona. From Tarragona the N240 goes to Poblet and on to Lérida. Nothing special in the way of hotels here, Ramon Berenguer IV in the Plaza named after the Catalan king is probably the best bet. Tel 23 73 45

Day 2   Lérida

Pons	70 k	43 m
Seo de Urgel	70 k	43 m
Andorra la Vella	20 k	12 m
Total	160 k	100 m

There is a good road C 1313 all the way to Seo de Urgel along the River Segre valley. You will see mountain scenery and it will be steep and winding as you approach Andorra. There is a modern Parador Nacional at Seo de Urgel Calle Santo Domingo. Tel 352 000. Alternatively there is the Roc Blanc at nearby Escaldes Tel: 21486.

Day 3   Andorra La Vella

Puigcerda	60 k	37 m
Ripoll	66 k	41 m

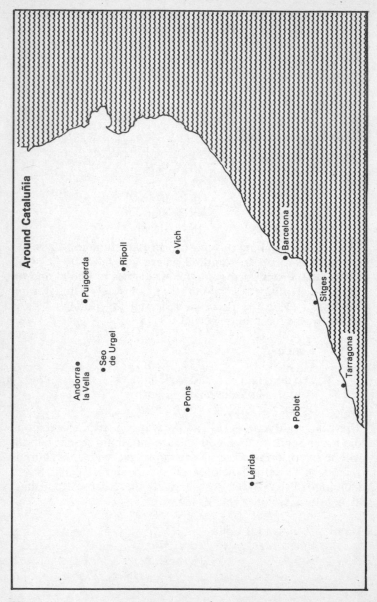

Around Cataluña

Puigcerda

Ripoll

Vich

Barcelona

Sitges

Tarragona

Andorra
la Vella

Seo
de Urgel

Pons

Poblet

Lérida

Vich	37 k	23 m
Barcelona	60 k	37 m
Total	223 k	139 m

You need to be prepared for steep climbs and sharp bends on the way to Puigcerda on the N20 across the French border. Then take the N152 to Ripol although the road remains steep with many bends much of it is down hill. The N152 continues improving. The grand old Ritz hotel in Gran Vía 668 Tel 318 52 00 has style and is pricey and the Oriente Ramblas 45/47 has atmosphere and is very reasonable at about £15 per night.

Chapter Three:
Historic Spain

During the years of the unification of Spain the vast, sparsely inhabited plateau that lies between the Cantabrian mountains and the Sierra de Gredos was the setting for dramas which could have been the inspiration for any number of Shakespeare's historical plays. Greed, rapacity, cruelty, idealism and double-dealing all featured in the strange and colourful period during which Spain became one of the most envied powers of the Western world. The relics of this extraordinary story, the castles – some of which have now become splendid paradors, the walled cities, the monasteries, the churches and the ancient houses all tell a story that makes a journey through this part of Spain endlessly rewarding.

In spring this is a green land burgeoning with new corn or with the grass on which the vast herds of livestock from the southern parts of the region are pastured. In summer the green turns to ochre, the same colour as the dusty villages, whose whitewashed houses look inwards into the streets and squares, almost invisible in the earth-coloured landscape. In winter there is snow, and a biting cold.

The river valleys remain green throughout the year, providing a welcome contrast to the plateau, and so do the mountain slopes of the Sierra de Gredos, just north of Madrid, and the southern slopes of the Montes Cantabricos on which herds of sheep have grazed since the times when the manufacture of wool was one of Europe's major industries. Most of the towns, cities and villages in this extensive region grew up round castles and monasteries where the lords and prince archbishops of medieval Spain held sway, scheming and fighting for the possession of lands. Their independent and quarrelsome principalities were easily overwhelmed when the united forces of Islam swept up the Iberian peninsula.

☆ ☆ ☆ ☆ ☆

The saga of Ferdinand and Isabella

For a traveller in Old Castile the romantic story of Ferdinand and Isabella, with its tragic aftermath, turns the austere landscape into a theatre of history. The walled towers, the forbidding castles, the golden buildings with their Isabelline decorations become the backdrop for one of the most fascinating stories of European history and help bring the past back to life for us today.

It was here, between the Cantabrian mountains and the Sierra de Gredos of the central cordillera, that the drama of the unification of Spain unfolded with acts of treachery, murder and mayhem that seem to have been inevitable during the early medieval evolution of the countries of Europe.

Isabella did not, as a child, expect to be queen. Juan II of Castile, her father, already had an heir, Henry, by his first wife, and another, her brother Alfonso, by his second wife, Isabel of Portugal, Isabella's mother. Her childhood at Madrigal de las Altas Torres, where she was born in 1451 was uneventful. Changes came when her father died and her half-brother became King Henry IV. Henry, who was an indecisive, impulsive and artistic man, suddenly exiled his stepmother and her family to Arévalo, near Avila. He was perhaps fearful that Isabel who was reputed to have caused the downfall and death of his father's adviser Don Alvaro de la Luna, might also plot against him to bring about the succession of her children.

Exile was no security against plots, however, and Henry soon decided to bring the children into his court while leaving their mother in isolation at Arévalo castle, where alone and deprived of her children she eventually lost her reason. Isabella was about eleven years old at the time and, having grown close to her mother during the years of exile, no doubt felt the separation keenly while also being alerted to the dangers of her own and her brother's position.

Meanwhile, Henry had married Juana of Portugal in the hope of fathering an heir who would prevent the crown passing to his half-brother or sister. In 1462 he announced that his wife had given him a daughter. This news was received with some scepticism by the feudal lords of Castile, whose contempt for Henry had been heightened by the licentiousness of his court and the wanton reputation of his new wife whose lover was known to be Henry's adviser Beltrán de la Cueva, Duke of Albuquerque. The new infant was soon known as 'La Beltraneja' and was ignored by influential and powerful forces in the kingdom, who began planning to make Alfonso the heir to the throne.

Alarmed by this turn of events, Henry gathered an army and a battle ensued at Olmedo. On the king's side were the Marquess of Santillana and Beltrán de la Cueva and, on Alfonso's, the warlike Bishop of Toledo, who went into battle with his episcopal cape over his armour, and another militant priest, the Bishop of Seville. The battle was inconclusive and the forces retired, those of the king to Medina del Campo and Alfonso's to Segovia where he and Isabella were reunited. It was then that tragedy struck. Hearing that the city of Toledo had turned against its Bishop, Alfonso and his army set off to the south but on the way he was suddenly taken ill and died; poisoned, according to some reports, by eating trout. He was thirteen years old.

The revolt against the King seemed doomed and Isabella and the Archbishop of Toledo were obliged to confirm their loyalty to Henry. There now followed a tussle during which Henry tried to neutralise Isabella's new role as heiress to the throne by marrying her off to the king of Portugal and, when that failed, to one of his feudal lords. At the same time the lords who supported

Isabella tried to persuade her to declare herself the rightful heir. With a surprising wisdom for a girl of fifteen Isabella resisted all commitments and, by her profession of loyalty to Henry, persuaded him to allow her to marry whom she chose and, moreover, to give her the towns of Avila, Medina del Campo, Olmedo, and Ubeda, in the south on the frontiers of the Moorish kingdom of Andalucía, as an acknowledgement that she was an heir to the throne.

With her position strengthened Isabella now contacted Ferdinand, heir to the throne of Aragon, through her supporters. The proposed union between the two prompted Henry, who hated the rival Christian kingdom, into instant action. He sent troops to the north of Castile to prevent the meeting of the young couple at Valladolid where Isabella had fled to wait for Ferdinand. Henry's move was ineffective however and Ferdinand, travelling quickly and in disguise, arrived at Valladolid for the fateful encounter with Isabella.

They hardly knew each other but these two young people – she was eighteen and he a year younger – had a common ambition: to unite Spain and eradicate the Moorish domination in the South. They were married in 1469. On the death of Henry IV, they were proclaimed sovereigns of Castile in 1474, and on the death of Ferdinand's father in 1479 the crowns of Castile and Aragon were united.

During their reigns Ferdinand and Isabella were constantly on the move, often separately, persuading their feudal lords to associate themselves with their crusade, planning attacks against Moorish cities and distributing newly conquered estates among their supporters, as well as dealing with the Cortes (parliaments) representing the various regions of Spain and drawing up the laws and regulations for their joint kingdoms. At the same time, Isabella was bearing children. Isabel, who married the Prince of Portugal; Juan, who died at the age of 19; Mary, who also married a Portuguese prince; and Juana who married

Philip the Handsome, heir to the Hapsburg kingdom of the Low Countries, Austria and Sicily. It was on this last marriage that Isabella and Ferdinand pinned their hopes for a unification of the great kingdoms of Europe.

The marriage, which seemed so full of promise, was a disaster. Philip carried his bride off to the Low Countries where he dismissed her Spanish attendants and occupied himself with political affairs and mistresses. Juana, who seems to have been a highly sensitive and artistic girl, became insanely jealous and unhappy, a state of mind made worse by the death of her mother in 1504 at Medina del Campo. Her life was in a crisis and there now began a long nightmare as her father and husband began to grapple for her inherited place as queen of Castile. The devious struggle between the two men came to an end with Philip's death at Burgos in 1506, which also caused another crisis in Juana's unstable life. In death Philip was once more hers alone and she took possession of his body with an obsessive fierceness. He was embalmed and kept in a private chapel where daily masses were said over him. Then she decided to move him to Granada. It was autumn and she was pregnant. The birth pains began at Torquemeda and there she gave birth to her last daughter, Catalina. Three months later the cortège moved on again but it was now winter and the meseta was bleak with snow and ice. There were more stops in tiny windswept villages, the coffin was wrapped in cattle skins, the cold was intense.

Meanwhile, Ferdinand was continuing his scheming to become king of Spain and also to outwit Spain's traditional enemies the French whose inroads into Italy threatened the Aragonese kingdom of Sicily and the commercial trade routes of the Mediterranean ports of Catalonia and Valencia. To Ferdinand the presence of Juana was inhibiting and an open invitation to unruly lords to oppose him so he banished her to his Tordesillas castle where she was a prisoner for 46 years.

During all the time she was incarcerated Juana swung from reason to insanity. Her visitors included her supporters as well as those of Ferdinand and conflicting reports were spread about the state of her mind. Some news was kept from her, like the death of her father in 1516. However with the arrival of her son Charles, who as Charles V became Holy Roman Emperor in 1516 as well as King Charles I of Spain she was once again a focal point of Spanish politics. There were those in Spain who resented being made an appendage of the Hapsburg Empire, with the taxation this implied as well as the funnelling of the wealth of the Spanish American Empire into the Hapsburg coffers. These protestors formed themselves into a movement called the **Comuneros** who were prepared to fight for their regional and Spanish rights and to do so by stating their allegiance to Juana and not to Charles.

Charles saw his mother during his visit to Spain. He visited her at Tordesillas with some of the Spanish lords and surprised her in her rooms, unkempt, bedraggled, a defeated woman. One can only imagine what went through his mind. The lords loyal to her rallied her, she was cleaned, dressed up and managed to make a speech about her willingness to serve her people. Charles, in his turn, declared the event a fraud and a charade. He gathered an army and defeated the Comunero resistance.

For Juana, this was the end. She deteriorated into an insane creature who crawled about her prison, her skin filthy and covered in sores. Her release came, with her death in April 1555. Later in that year her son Charles, Holy Roman Emperor, ruler of Spain, the Low Countries, Austria, Milan, Sicily and Spanish America, abdicated and divided his kingdom between his brother Ferdinand and son Philip. Charles retired for what remained of his life to the monastery of Yuste in Extremadura.

☆ ☆ ☆ ☆ ☆

In old Castile

Though old Castile stretches up to the Cantabrian mountains, in this chapter I am looking at the region south of the Road to Santiago (see Chapter Nine).

In this region are some of the oldest and most evocative towns in Spain. Here the remains of the original, ancient towns form the nucleus of the new towns that grew around them in later periods and that are still growing fast today as the new Spain expands its industrial potential. Some of the towns still retain their medieval walls almost intact, others have large sections of them embedded in later buildings, and all of them contain magnificent religious buildings and lordly town mansions. Now as in the past, the centre of their social life is in the Plaza Mayor, the main square, always complete with colonnades, fountains, bars and cafés to provide focal points for Spanish society.

The roads and railways connecting these towns and cities radiate from Madrid and there is a network of minor roads connecting the main national highway so most of the places mentioned in this chapter are easy to reach, some of them being close enough for a day excursion from Madrid.

Nearest and most dramatic of these cities is **Segovia**, 91 km (56 miles) from Madrid, and with a motorway (**autopista**) for more than half the distance. There are also numerous coach and train services between the two cities every day.

The first view you will glimpse of Segovia, if you approach from the east, is stunning. The wedge-shaped spur of hill on which the town stands is crowned at this eastern end by the castle, a fantastic vision of stone rising from the valleys of the Rivers Eresma and Clamores to slate-covered roofs and pinnacles which evoke every illustration of a castle ever published in books of Grimms' Fairy Tales. True, most of this great view was remodelled in the 19th century when the original castle was gutted by fire, but this seems irrelevant as you admire the soaring lines of the present building outlined against the blue sky.

Old Castile

● Valladolid

● Zamora   ● Toro   ● Tordesillas

● Medina
del Campo

Madrigal
de las Altas Torres
●   ● Arévalo

● Salamanca

● Segovia

● El Escorial

● Madrid

The original castle, or **Alcázar**, was built in the 14th century and rebuilt by Isabella's father, Juan II. It was here that Isabella learned that she was to be Queen and it remained a royal residence until after her death. Some of this original building remains, though it was refurbished in the 19th century. The keep is also attributed to Juan II, though Philip II added the slate roofs.

The rooms you see today, though rebuilt, evoke the atmosphere of the originals and the furnishings, some of which are medieval, add to the effect. In the King's Rooms (**Sala de los Reyes**) and Queen's Dressing Room (**El Tocador de la Reina** you are standing in the part of the palace which predates Juan II. Rooms from his period include the large north hall, La Galera, and The Pines (**Las Pinas**). The general effect of the Alcázar is one of make-believe, despite the authenticity of some of its contents, such as the cannons and armour. It certainly spurs the imagination as much as, or more than, some ancient buildings preserved in their original state.

Outside the entrance to the Alcázar is a pleasant wooded square from which photographers with zoom lenses capture images of the church of the True Cross (**Vera Cruz**) and the **Monasterio del Parral** without having to go to the trouble of walking across the Eresma valley. The first is a church founded by the Knights Templar in the 13th century and is well worth a closer inspection by anyone interested in the Romanesque style for it is modelled on the Holy Sepulchre in Jerusalem and has some 13th-century wall paintings. The monastery was built by Isabella's half brother, King Henry IV, and has some fine stone carvings.

Inland along the spur of hill from the Alcázar is the old town of Segovia whose narrow streets retain some medieval houses and churches that provide plenty of interest for the casual stroller. Many of the houses have painted and incised plaster work known as 'esgrafiado' and several have attractive courtyards. Look out for the one that belonged to the **Marques del Arco** and the **Casa de Hierro**, with its highly decorated gate. Also, interesting are the Tower of the Lozoyas, (**Torreon de Lozoyas**), which belonged to powerful

Segovian families who liked to keep an eye out for their enemies, and the **Casa de los Picos**, so-named because of the pointed stones in its facade.

The latter is in the Plaza San Martin by the 12th-century church of the same name the house of **Juan Bravo**, one of the Comuneros who rebelled against Charles V and died as the hero of a futile resistance. His statue is in the square. Churches abound in the old town – as, of course, they do everywhere in Spain after so many centuries of priestly power. Among these are the Romanesque churches of Holy Trinity (**Santa Trinidad**); St Stephen (**San Esteban**), which has a six-storeyed spire; and St John of the Knights, (**San Juan de los Caballeros**) which now houses the studio of Daniel Zuloaga, a 19th century potter who did much to revive this traditional Spanish craft.

The dominant religious building in old Segovia is the **Cathedral**, the original of which was destroyed during the revolt of the Comuneros. Having defeated them, Charles V either as a generous gesture or to gain public approval, had the cathedral rebuilt in the 16th century and his architects did a good job. The building is in a honey-coloured stone and has a gothic elegance which has given it the title of the Lady of Spanish cathedrals. Its interior, with soaring pillared columns and interwoven stone decorations on the vaults, has a great beauty enhanced by the wrought iron, gilded grilles of the chapels which contain paintings and alterpiees. The cloisters with their groined vaults, rebuilt on a new site by Jose Campero, provide a tranquil break between seeing the cathedral and a visit to the chapter house which has many paintings and objects by well-known masters.

The spur of hill on which Segovia stands has a dip on which the Romans built an impressive **aqueduct** which rivals the Alcázar and Cathedral as a point of interest. It was probably built in the time of Hadrian, a Spanish Roman from near Seville, and it is still in use though today the water runs in pipes through it.

Below it is the **Plaza Azoquejo**, a busy place with plenty of traffic and many cafés and restaurants. One of these restaurants is the famous **Mesón del Candido** which despite becoming something of a tourist haunt has lost none of its excellence. Its lamb and roast kid done in the Segovian style are memorable. Other restaurants nearby worth visiting are **El Cordero** and **La Criolla**.

To the south-west of Segovia and less than 30 k (20 miles) away is **Avila**. Your first sight of this town is almost as breathtaking as that of Segovia, especially if you approach it on the Salamanca road.

From here, the 2.5 k (1.5 miles) of perfect walls with their 88 towers make a wonderful sight across the fields. As you are at a higher level than the town, you will have a fine view of the roof tops of the houses huddling together inside the walls for protection. The roofs rise towards the Cimorro, the low hill on which stands the Cathedral, a building which is half church and half fortress with its apse forming one of the defensive towers of the wall. The **Cathedral** has two facades, one with two towers, one of which is incomplete and the other of which is called the Apostles facade; built in the 13th century, the latter later acquired baroque additions.

The interior of the cathedral mixes an interesting variety of architectural styles, including Romanesque, Renaissance and Baroque. The building is in red and white grained marble which creates an unusual effect in the light which streams in from the high windows in the nave. The nine chapels have tombs, altar paintings and sculptures. Of particular interest are the 15th-century madonna, and a 12th century Romanesque panel. Isabella must have known the cathedral and certainly knew the Romanesque church of St Vincent (**San Vicente**) which is a fine, solid building with some outstanding carvings on its west portal. The church lies in the north-east corner of the town just outside the walls on the site where Vicente of Huesca and his two sisters were martyred. The canopied tomb of the saints is in the church and is decorated with bas reliefs showing episodes in their lives.

Since Avila played an important part in Isabella's life she and Ferdinand endowed the monastery of Saint Thomas (**Santo Tomas**) which lies outside the town. The church is dedicated to St Thomas Aquinas, the great medieval scholar who was born near Aquino, Italy, and the altarpiece by

75

Pedro de Berruguete recounts the story of the saint's life. There are three important tombs in the church, including that of the young prince Juan, only son of Ferdinand and Isabella. The tomb was carved by the Florentine sculptor Fancelli who also made the tomb of the Catholic Monarchs in the Capilla Real at Seville. An interesting detail of the architecture of Saint Thomas is the use of arrows and yokes as decorative features; the first letter of the Spanish word for these artefacts, **Flecha** and **Yugo**, are also the first letters of the names of the Catholic Monarchs (Y being used for I in medieval times).

Avila is also renowned as the birthplace of that high flying saint, **Teresa of Avila**, who, to her intense discomfort and embarrassment, was given the gift of levitation – according to legend, anyway. Prosaic fact records that her real claim to fame was the remarkable influence for good she had on the lax standards of the Catholic Church in the 16th century when wealthy monasteries and convents were succumbing to materialistic temptations. Her main success was with the Carmelites, for whom she re-established traditional disciplines and created 17 new convents.

Three of Teresa's convents in Avila can be visited today, including the Convent of the Saint (**Convento de la Santa**), built on the estate belonging to her well-to-do parents and which contains relics and paintings of her life, the **Convent of La Encarnación** and The Convent of **St Joseph**, also called Las Madres.

Some 99 k (60 miles) from Avila to the north-west along the N501 lies **Salamanca**, the great university city which was an important centre of learning from the 13th century onwards. Having existed since before Roman times, Salamanca played a part in the Carthaginian wars when Hannibal held it for a time. The Romans regarded it as a place of strategic importance, though today there is little evidence of their occupation, except for the bridge across the River Tormes. After the Roman retreat and the arrival of the Visigoths this part of Spain became a battleground fought over by rival local warlords known here as 'Los Bandos'. These bands of medieval ruffians spread havoc among the country people on whom they preyed. Their battles with rival families were fought with utter ruthlessness and sometimes entire families were decapitated, a fate the Monroys meted out to the Manzanos. This kind of behaviour, not uncommon in medieval Europe, subsided with the establishment of law and order once Spain was unified. Peace also brought a new life to Salamanca whose educational establishments began to be patronised by some of the highest families in the land. Its famous sons included Pope Benedict XIII, Don Juan, son of Isabella, Fray Luis de Leon, and St John of the Cross.

The patronage of wealthy families brought wealth to Salamanca and led to the building of the churches and noble mansions which are the pride of the city today.

The original base of the University was the **Old Cathedral**, built at the river end of the town and to which was added the **New Cathedral**.

The Old Cathedral, though overwhelmed by the size and height of the New, is a fascinating building. From the outside an unassuming structure, though its Cock Tower (**Torre del Gallo**) with its tiled roof and two tiers of windows is notable, inside the building is outstanding. The design is a simple Latin Cross with two aisles and a transept, the north end of which connects with the New Cathedral. In the transepts and crossing, which rises to the Cock Tower, are several 13th-15th century carved tombs set in decorated niches and in the chapels are many interesting paintings and sculptures from the same period. The jewel of these works of art is the huge 15th-century reredos, the 53 panels which depict the lives of Jesus and the Virgin, and which is topped by a fresco of the Last Judgement by Nicolas Fiorentino. In this, Christ and his Angels in white robes dominate the crowds of the saved, and those condemned to eternal damnation are shown naked as was the medieval custom. Standing before the reredos is a rather lovely statue of the Virgen de la Vega, the patron saint of Salamanca.

The New Cathedral is splendidly ornate in a Gothic and Plateresque style and its facade decorated with Churrigueresque features, is richly embellished with carvings. Above it rises a forest of towers and pinnacles topped by a central dome and marked, at its eastern end, by a tall tower built in imitation of the Giralda of Seville. In the interior, which soars up to a star-vaulted ceiling, is the enclosed choir common to Spanish churches. This choir is designed by the Churriguera brothers Joaquin and Alberto and has ornately carved choir stalls. More Churriguera work can be seen in the area behind the choir and in the Chapel of the Battles (**Capilla de las Batallas**) with its elaborate reredos. The 11th-century crucifix carried by El Cid on his campaigns is kept in the chapel.

Opposite the western end of the New Cathedral is **The University of Salamanca** housed in a building with an outstanding Plateresque facade embellished with the arms of Ferdinand and Isabella and flanked by ornate pillars. Through the gateway you walk into the attractive colonnaded Patio de las Escuelas Menores where, on one of the columns, is a good luck token for students at the University – a frog mounted on three skulls. To the left of the entrance to the patio is the lecture room of Fray Luis Leon, whose humanist ideas got him into trouble with the Inquisition who arrested him. When he was released, he simply returned to the university and continued the lecture which had been interrupted with the words 'As I was saying'.

Churches, convents, monasteries and mansions abound in Salamanca – too many to describe in detail here. The following are of particular interest. By the university is the **House of Alvarez Abarca** where you will find the Salamanca Museum which contains archaeology and fine arts departments. Next to it is the Students' Hospice (**Hospital del Estudio**), a 16th-century hospice in the Gothic style and nearby is the house where Miguel de Unamuno, the distinguished philosopher, author and independent thinker, lived. He was jailed for being a Republican and died in 1936 at the beginning of the Civil War. His house is now a museum devoted to his life and work.

Walking up the Calle Mayor from the cathedral you come to one of the most memorable houses in Salamanca, the **Casa de las Conchas**. It was built in 1512 for the Maldonado family who advertised their loyalty to the order of Santiago de

Compostela by covering their house in carved shells, the symbols of St James. Across the street is the **Church of La Clericia**, a typical 18th-century baroque building with two towers outside and an ornate gilded reredos inside. Continuing along the Calle Mayor, you will come to the Romanesque church of **San Martin** and then reach the **Plaza Mayor**. One of the finest town squares in Spain, it was built according to Philip V's instructions in the same style as the Plaza Mayor in Madrid and is largely the work of the Churriguera brothers. Like most main squares, this one is a busy place with shops and cafés behind the colonnades providing delightful stopping places after a morning's sightseeing. After a rest you may be inspired to stroll along the Calle Prior from the western end of the Plaza Mayor to the Plaza de Agustinas and the Calle de las Ursulinas to see more of the honey-coloured buildings which gave Salamanca the name of La Dorada, the Golden City.

On the eastern side of the city are more buildings worth looking at, especially the two convents of **San Esteban** and **Las Dueñas**, both reached from the New Cathedral along Calle del Tostado. The former has a sculptured facade under the huge arch of its front and the latter a beautiful cloister.

Sixty-five kilometres (40 miles) to the north of Salamanca lies **Zamora**, famous for its Romanesque buildings, and about the same distance to the east of this town, is **Valladolid**. In the square of countryside between Arévalo and these cities lie the smaller towns where much of the drama of the early years of Isabella unfolded.

Madrigal de las Altas Torres, on the C 610 off the Avila-Salamanca road, is a sleepy town with the walls and gates that Isabella knew still standing in a protective circle about the old houses. The palace of the kings of Castile in which Isabella was born is still there, though it is now the Convent of Augustinian Mothers of Our Lady of Grace, (**Convento de Madres Agustinas de Nuestra Señora de Gracia**), given to them by Charles V. Also surviving is the church of **San Nicolas de Bari**, a 12th-century building at which Isabella undoubtedly worshipped.

To the east, on the road from Madrid to the north-west, is

Arévalo. The castle where Isabella's mother was exiled has disappeared, though a 14th-century palace, furnished in 16th-century style, still exists. Arévalo also has several 14th-century churches which, no doubt, Isabella knew. Chief of these is **San Martin**, built in Mudéjar style and with its two imposing square towers overlooking a large unpaved plaza, usually showing little life except a few stray animals and some people gathered under the porticoes of the village bar.

This is typical of the small towns of Old Castile, many of them deserted by the young who have gone to earn their living elsewhere because they see little hope of an improvement in their lives if they stay. Nevertheless, for the visitor there are some rewards in the silence and emptiness of these places where the stillness seems to suggest time has stopped. It is as if you have stepped into a time warp in which the evidence of the past and the actuality of the present seem to merge and evaporate in the burning sunshine reflected off the dry earth.

From Arévalo the road goes north to **Medina del Campo** where Isabella died. The **Castle of La Mota** still stands here around its great keep built on older foundations and improved in 1440 by Juan II and with the coats of arms of Ferdinand and Isabella added in 1482. The centre of the town is the Plaza de España where the brick Town Hall, with balconies and wrought-iron work, is to be found and there is the small place where Isabella died. Once one of the great trade fair towns of Spain, Medina del Campo is a quiet place today. It livens up during the annual sheep fair when the atmosphere evokes the great fairs of the time when the lords of the Mesta ruled Castile and controlled all the sheep routes and, thus, the great medieval wool trade.

Continuing along the road to the north from Medina del Campo, you reach **Tordesillas**. The castle where the wretched Juana was imprisoned for 46 long years and went mad has long since disappeared, but not all traces of her have gone. In the Royal Monastery of Saint Clair (**Real Monasterio de Santa Clara**), is an organ she played and clavichord decorated with Flemish paintings. The Convent also held memories of Pedro the Cruel who resided here at about the time that he called on the Black Prince for help against the French. Incidentally the Black Prince's reward was the ruby that now features in the State Crown of Britain.

In this historic and embattled region are many castles. One of the most outstanding is **Simancas**, near Valladolid, once a Moorish stronghold and which became in Philip II's reign the General Archive of Spain, a role which it still performs today by preserving some 30 million documents. Another, rather unusual castle is **Coca** built in Mudéjar style by the Moors to the orders of Bishop Don Alonso Fonseca. The entirely brick building is protected by a moat. A third interesting castle lies at **Cuellar**, to the north-east of Coca. It was built by Beltrán de la Cuevas, Duke of Albuquerque and lover of Juana of Portugal. Surrounded by a wall with four towers, the castle has a galleried courtyard and several handsome panelled rooms.

Though most of the towns that played such an important role in the lives of Ferdinand and Isabella and their family are now neglected and almost forgotten, this is not the case with **Valladolid** where they were married.

Valladolid is a university town and episcopal See on the River Pisuerga. It is also an industrial city which has developed haphazardly and in which there has been much destruction of its old quarters. Nevertheless, something remains of the buildings that Ferdinand and Isabella built or that were built during their lifetime. The most interesting of these is the **Colegio San Gregorio**, a religious college founded by Isabella's confessor Fray Alonso de Burgos which is notable for its Isabelline style of architecture. Once you have seen the gateway of this college the meaning of the Isabelline style becomes instantly clear. The intricate and delicate work which characterises this style is recognizable as the forerunner of the Plateresque style which was to follow and which can be seen in the galleried balcony of the inner courtyard. The building is also interesting for its fusion of several styles, including the Gothic, seen in the stairway balustrades and the Mudejar style of the panellings.

Today, San Gregorio houses the National Museum of Polychrome sculpture, and also contains baroque works and paintings. To northern sensibilities there is something suspect about those polychrome painted effigies, encountered again and again in Spanish churches, with their realistic and melodramatic expressions, the sugary serenity of the madonnas and the bleeding wounds of Christ crucified. But perhaps we should be a little more tolerant of these ikons. They personify concepts of idealism and suffering just as real to the sensibilities of ordinary Spanish people as a painting of the death of Nelson once conveyed the idea of heroism to the Victorians. The realism of the figures and the quality of the wood carving is often beyond criticism and for this reason, if for no other, they are worth looking at. Among the polychrome artists of high repute are Alonso Berruguete, Juan de Juni and Gregorio Fernandez.

Facing San Gregorio is the church of St Paul (**San Pablo**) built by Simon of Cologne (**Simon de Colonia**) who was also involved in the architecture of Burgos Cathedral. Philip II, who was born in Valladolid, was baptised in this church. Its facade is Isabelline with a mixture of Gothic and inside are the tombs of several early lords of Castile.

The centre of Valladolid lies a few streets away to the south between the cathedral and the Plaza Mayor, a traditional colonnaded square. There is always a good deal of movement in this part of the city for the University lies near the Cathedral and the streets and cafés are thronged with students during term time.

The Cathedral, commissioned by Philip II from his architect Herrera, actually took some 300 years to reach its present state and it cannot be denied that the various styles and additions that occurred during that time did not lead to the harmonious whole. The facade is still incomplete, with only one tower instead of the two that were planned. However, the interior, with its simple but powerful Herrera design, makes an impressive effect heightened by the reredos of Juan de Juni, which was originally made for the Church of **Santa María La Antigua**, a Romanesque church in Calle de Marques del Duero. Other paintings and sculptures of the cathedral, including two paintings by Velasquez, can be seen in the museum of works of art attached to the church.

Among the many churches and noble palaces in Valladolid, one simple house has a particular appeal to the visitor – the house in which **Cervantes** spent his last years. It is an unpretentious place with furniture and tapestries from Cervantes' time providing another side of the picture of the Golden Age.

The Central Cordillera

Some 60 kilometres (37 miles) to the south of Salamanca there rise a range of sierras which, with the River Tagus, make a natural defensive wall between the region of Extremadura and old Castile. At the western end near the Portuguese frontier these mountains are called the Sierra de la Peña de Francia: the central section, the Sierra de Gredos; and the range that passes north of Madrid, the Sierra de Guadarrama. In the past these ranges which form the Central Range (Cordillera Central) were a barrier against the Moors and an obstacle in Wellington's campaign against the French armies of Napoleon. Today they are a beautiful and unspoilt refuge from the summer heat and drought of the central meseta as well as a haven for wild life.

At the western end of the sierras lies the hilltop town of **Ciudad Rodrigo**, its outline dominated by the square tower of the Alcázar, fought over by Moors, Spaniards, and the French who held it against Wellington. The ramparts of this town fortress provide a stirring sightseeing walk, and the 12th-century church of **San Fernando** is of interest. Added to at various periods, it has many fine features, not least being the carved capitals and tympanum which are fine examples of medieval figure carving. In contrast is the rather austere classical chapel in the style of Herrera, the **Capilla del Carralbo** which contains paintings by Ribera.

The **Alcázar** itself, a square powerful-looking building, is now the **Parador Nacional Enrique II**. It is an ideal base for those wishing to stay in this attractive town, whose market days in the Plaza Mayor are a highlight of a visit.

To the east of Ciudad Rodrigo is **La Alberca**, a small village of stone houses and overhanging roofs which mark it as a mountain community of farmers and shepherds. Near it rises the highest mountain of the range, the Peña de Francia (1732 m 5682 ft). The Peña rises steeply, providing wide-ranging views over the meseta of Castile as far as Salamanca.

Further west begin the Sierra de Gredos whose highest point is Almanzor (2592 m 8502 ft). This is a popular area for climbers and those who enjoy caves for the Cuevas del Aguila are open to the public and provide a subterranean spectacle of stalactites, stalagmites and streams of crystalline rocks.

To preserve the natural beauty, and the flora and fauna of this region, a Gredos National Park (**Reserva Nacional de Gredos**) has been formed. There is a parador perched high up among pine trees and the mountain scenery presents a startling contrast to the dry meseta below.

The Guadarrama range begins at the Pass of Guadarrama near the Escorial and provides Madrileños with a land of mountains, forests and greenery which comes as a welcome relief from the summer heat of the capital. There are several mountain resorts that you can use as bases for walking and fishing in the summer and skiing in winter. Among these are: the Lion Heights (**Alto de los Leones**) at the summit of the Guadarrama Pass at the western end; **Puerta de Navacerrada** (1860 m 7102 ft) a superb viewpoint and popular winter sports resort, and the nearby **Puerta de las Cotos** (1830 m 6004 ft) at the summit of a ski hoist from which you can walk to Lake Peñalara. Though the sierras are places to visit for their natural beauty there are also two places of historic interest in the Guadarrama: the **Monasterio del Paular**, the first Carthusian monastery in Spain, whose monastic buildings round a cloister are now a hotel, and the **Valle de los Caidos**, the spectacular monument dreamed up by General Franco to commemorate the dead of the Civil War. A lovely valley surrounded by granite crags was the setting for this gesture towards reconciliation. Its focal point is a basilica carved out of a rocky crag above which stands a gigantic cross. The nave is 262 m (860 ft) long, greater than St Peters in Rome, and is flanked by chapels with Brussels tapestries and alabaster copies of all the leading madonnas of Spain. A **tour de force** if ever there was one and a reminder that places in which the human spirit resides are not built in a day or by carefully thought-out design.

☆ ☆ ☆ ☆ ☆

Wellington in Old Castile

Wellington's Peninsular Campaign is one of the epics of military history and a knowledge of some of its details adds much to the interest of a journey in old Castile. It was here that some of the major victories were won, driving the French and Joseph Bonaparte back into France and liberating Spain. The towns and cities, the rivers and mountains in which the battles were fought, are still there. With a little imagination you can people the landscape with Wellington's red-coated British troops, Scottish Highlanders and Irish Rangers as well as the colourful and dashing French Chasseurs and Dragoons.

The peninsular campaign was not an easy one for General Arthur Wellesley, later Lord Wellington. He landed in Portugal in 1809 and advanced into Spain where he won a victory at Talavera in July 1809, against Marshal Victor, which served mainly to alert the French to the threat of his invasion. A great French army, with such men as Marshals Massena, Soult, Marmont and Ney at its head now gathered to attack him.

There was only one thing to do and that was to retreat. Wellesley had constructed the famous lines of Torres Vedras across the peninsula north of the Tagus at Lisbon and it was here that he waited until he received reinforcements and the spring arrived.

Massena followed him towards Lisbon, sure at first that he would sweep Wellesley and his army into the sea, but he soon realised that the lines were impregnable and so he too sat down to wait. However it was winter, Massena was far from his base, his troops were falling ill and there was not enough food so he in his turn began to retreat towards Madrid. Wellesley now took the initiative, following Massena to the Spanish border. In May 1811 a battle took place at **Fuentes de Oroño** where Massena had returned to free the French fortress of **Almeida** on the Portuguese side of the border. The battle fluctuated round the little village with the day almost lost but Wellesley's calm control turned a desperate situation into victory. It was a costly one, however, with 1545 dead against the French 2192.

To consolidate his victory and advance into Spain Wellesley needed to take the two key cities of **Ciudad Rodrigo** and **Badajoz**. By 8 January 1812 Wellesley was ready for the siege of Ciudad Rodrigo. Trenches were dug in the frozen ground along the River Aguedo and a bombardment to breach the walls began. The attack up the steep slopes towards the Alcazar was carried out with desperate speed and there was much hand-to-hand fighting led by the Irish Connaught Rangers as the town was stormed and sacked. Drunken troops took over the town and looting, rape and murder could not be stopped even by those brave and humane officers who tried; very often by attacking their own frenzied soldiers with rifle butts.

The siege of Badajoz was an even more hazardous venture and prompted Wellesley for the first time to mutter the famous phrase about 'a close run thing' attributed to Waterloo. It began on 16 March and six days later the rain arrived, turning the River Guadiana into a raging torrent which swept away the pontoon bridge that the engineers had built and filled the trenches with water. To make matters worse, Wellesley heard that Marshal Marmont was marching on Ciudad Rodrigo. Aware of his precarious position and shortage of troops Wellesley nevertheless continued the siege and on 6 April, Easter Sunday gave the order to attack the heavily fortified town above the river.

Once again there was bloody and terrible hand-to-hand fighting. The advance guard finding the wall lined with swords, pushed their comrades against the sharp blades, using their bodies as a bridge over the steel and at last the town fell and suffered the fate of all too many towns that failed to surrender. Buildings were burned, nuns and children were bayonetted, as the fear of the battle which the men felt before the attack turned into the savagery of victory.

Secure now with his two frontier fortress towns, Wellesley turned his attention to his campaign. Soult was in the south based in Seville and Marmont was at Salamanca.

As usual, Wellesley did not reveal his intentions for he knew how quickly information passed on to the enemy. On 17 June, however, he was at Salamanca where Marmont had left a garrison. Within ten days the garrison had surrendered. Wellesley and his army relaxed in the Plaza Mayor. He and his officers were feted by the high-ranking Spanish families while his men made the most of their opportunities with the common people. During the next month the two armies watched each other and manoeuvred for positions south of Salamanca. Marmont attempted to cut Wellesley's communication with Ciudad Rodrigo and Wellesley in his turn was determined that this should not happen. Marmont moved on to the hills called the Greater Arapiles and Wellesley occupied the Lesser. While watching Marmont's troops Wellesley suddenly realised that the French lines had become over extended and seized the opportunity. Ordering his brother-in-law Packenham to advance under cover of some undulating ground he surprised a French division and caused severe losses, including the capture of a large number of cannon. Though the fighting continued the battle had in fact been won.

Wellington, as he now became, moved to Madrid and it was there that Goya painted the portrait now in London's National Gallery. It's a superb image of the stubborn, self disciplined autocratic, the man who knew exactly what he wanted and what he expected from others. After Salamanca Wellington knew that he was master of Spain. His hard-won victories in Castile opened up the way to subsequent victories, notably at Vitoria and San Sebastian and led to the end of French rule in Spain.

☆ ☆ ☆ ☆ ☆

Motoring itinerary

Day 1	Madrid	
	Escorial	49 k 30 m
	Avila	109 k 68 m
	Total	158 k 98 m

Leave Madrid on the motorway for Villacastin. Take detour to Escorial.

Exit to Avila on the N501.

Stay at Parador Raimondo de Borgoña, Calle Marques de Canales y Chozas, Tel 21 13 40, once a 15th century palace of the Benavides, by the northern section of the walls of Avila. Or the Palacio de Valderrabanos by the Cathedral, Tel. 21 10 23.

Day 2	Avila	
	Salamanca	99 k 61 m
	Zamora	65 k 40 m
	Total	164 k 102 m

Take the N501 to Salamanca then the N630 to Zamora. Stay at Parador Condes de Alba y de Aliste. The remains of the 15th century palace include a splendid courtyard with arcades on two floors. There is also a swimming pool. Plaza Canovas Tel. 51 44 97.

Day 3	Zamora	
	Toro	33 k 20 m
	Tordesillas	33 k 20 m
	Simancas Castle	20 k 12 m
	Valladolid	10 k 6 m
	Total	96 k 60 m

The N122 from Zamora goes east to Toro and then Tordesillas. Here you take the N620 to Valladolid passing

Simancas castle. There is a modern parador at Tordesillas, Tel. 77 00 51, with a swimming pool and near Simancas there is a converted farmhouse called El Montico, on the route. In Valladolid the Olid Melia, Plaza de San Miguel, is one of a good standard chain of hotels.

Day 4	Valladolid		
	Medina del Campo	47 k	29 m
	Madrigal de las Altas		
	Torres	25 k	15 m
	Arévalo	25 k	15 m
	Segovia	70 k	43 m
	Total	91 k	57 m

From Valladolid a secondary road C610 goes to Medina del Campo and the same road continues to Madrigal de las Torres. From here the C605 goes to Arévalo and crossing the main road to Madrid NV1 goes on to Segovia. There are plenty of places to stay in Segovia and Los Linajes, Dr Velasco 9 Tel. 43 12 01, in the old part is full of charm and very popular. The Parador Nacional de Segovia is out of town on the road to Valladolid. It is modern and has a swimming pool, Tel 430 462

Day 5	Segovia		
	Madrid	91 k	56 m
	Total	91 k	57 m

You will be spoilt for choice as regards hotels in Madrid. The expensive but charismatic Ritz costs about treble what you will pay in the other hotels suggested in these routes but once or twice on a holiday you might wish to enjoy the undoubted pleasures of luxurious hotels. (About £70 a night). Plaza de la Lealtad Tel 221 2857. Another more modest grande dame, though with all mod. cons. is the Victoria, Plaza del Angel Tel 231 4500

Chapter Four:
Madrid's treasure trove

As cities go, Madrid is not very old, most of the buildings in its so-called 'old' quarter dating back to no earlier than the 18th century. However, the age of a city is not only counted in years; there is something about the life and experience of a people that adds a patina to the places where they lived, and so it is with Spain's capital.

Madrid, like Spain itself, grew up the hard way, having to face the challenge of foreign occupation by an alien people before finding its national identity. Due to the Moorish occupation and the spirit of the Reconquista the growth of Spain was austere, purposeful and disciplined. The single-minded resolution of Ferdinand and Isabella, the Inquisition, and the earnest dedication of Philip II forced on Spain an immediate adulthood in which there was little room for the gaiety found in other cultures. It was Philip who made Madrid his capital and imbued it with his spirit. In 16th-century, and 17th-century Spain life was formal and sombre with far less of that light-hearted spirit reflected in the plays of Shakespeare in England or the gusto of a Villon or Rabelais in France.

Dynastic influences

The Hapsburg reign in Spain came to an end in 1700 when the Bourbons inherited the Spanish throne through the will of Charles II, who left no heir but appointed Philip, Duke of Anjou, grandson of Louis XIV, as his successor. This prompted the War of the Spanish Succession as the great powers of Europe divided their support between the Austrian and French claimants to the Spanish throne. The

Bourbons, who were related to the Hapsburgs, Spain's previous dynasty, through Maria Theresa wife of Charles V, won the day and the Bourbon ascendancy in Spain began with Philip V. The Spain that Philip inherited was bankrupt and demoralised and, though a frivolous young man, Philip soon set about trying to improve things. Among his tasks he undertook to refurbish his capital city which, compared to the French cities that he knew, was unbearably sombre and uncared for. To a great extent it is his and his successors' architecture that makes up some of the noteworthy buildings of Madrid today. The Bourbons, used to the life of the French court, also attempted to inspire the society of Madrid with the elegance and style of France but with less success. However, Charles III and, after the Napoleonic wars, Ferdinand VII managed to gain support for the conversion of the Prado, originally built in 1785 as a Natural History museum, into one of the best collections of art in the world.

The Bourbon influence on Madrid was shortlived. Despite their weak attempts to pacify Napoleon, Joseph Bonaparte replaced Charles IV as King of Spain in 1808, only to be driven out by Wellington in 1812. Joseph did find time to create some of the grand boulevards and open spaces which still give distinction to the capital before he fled.

Throughout the 19th century Madrid was a focal point of internal wars; the three Carlist wars which were essentially between conservative and progressive elements finally brought about the abdication of Isabel II, daughter of Ferdinand VII and the declaration of a republic in 1868. The republic proved shortlived and the struggle continued into the 20th century, finally bringing about another abdication, that of Alfonso XIII, and then the civil war which produced the Franco era (1939 to 1975).

Throughout all these vicissitudes Madrid itself seems to have altered little until the post-Franco era under King Juan Carlos. Until then life in Madrid was what H.V. Morton in his book **A Stranger in Spain** calls 'charmingly Victorian'; today it is changing rapidly to conform with the style of the other capitals of Europe.

The Puerta del Sol and old Madrid

The heart of Madrid is the Gateway of the Sun (**Puerta del Sol**) an untidy, well-worn square where since time immemorial men have gathered at the innumerable bars to drink, nibble at tapas, discuss business or talk about bullfighting, politics or women. Today, of course, this is also a gathering place for the liberated Spanish woman and for tourists, but much of the chauvinist male atmosphere persists, especially in the more scruffy bars with their gruff, energetic counter waiters and their smell of fried fish and cigarette smoke. Puerta del Sol is not only the sentimental heart of the city but literally the crossroads of most of its means of communication. Here ten streets converge on the lozenge-shaped square as well as three metro lines and many bus routes.

From Puerta del Sol the Calle Mayor heads West towards the Royal Palace (**Palacio Nacional**) through the oldest quarter of Madrid. Though Calle Mayor is no longer the main street its name suggests, it still has a grandee air about it and in its vicinity are some of Madrid's most attractive restaurants such as Casa Ciriaco and Casa Botín in Cuchilleros (where Ernest Hemingway used to eat, but don't let that put you off).

The **Plaza Mayor** just off the Calle, was once the place where bullfights and auto da fés at which heretics were judged and condemned took place. Today, it is the scene of less lurid happenings such as political meetings, concerts and festivals and when there are no major events there are usually entertainers walking around playing guitars, doing mime shows, or performing acrobatic tricks. It is a place that is just as popular with Madrileños as with tourists and there are plenty of cafés, wine bodegas and bars.

In the centre of the square is an equestrian statue of Philip III. He was the feeble minded son of Anne of Austria and Philip II. The sad result of the misguided inbreeding tradition of the Hapsburgs, which ignored the fact that Philip II's grandmother was Juana la Loca.

The striking building on the north side of the square is the **Casa de la Panadería** so called because a bakery once stood here, and to the south is the knife makers street **Cuchilleros** which leads into a maze of narrow streets full of small restaurants and bodegones, mesones and cavas and to Calle Toledo, a long street with unusual shops in which is the 17th century former Jesuit School, the **Church of San Isidro**, patron saint of Madrid. Past the church a left fork takes you down the Ribera de los Curtidores where the famous **Rastro** market operates on Sundays. Like most markets that have become internationally known the Rastro is more a place to go for fun and to watch other people than for finding bargains. You will find every imaginable item from trombones to toast racks laid out on the stalls. It's an amusing way to spend Sunday morning but watch out for pickpockets.

Further west of the Plaza Mayor is the City Square (**Plaza de la Villa**) around which are some of the oldest houses in Madrid. The most interesting of them is the Town Hall (**Ayuntamiento** built in 1640 by Gomez de Mira, who also designed the Plaza Mayor. Another is the Lujan Tower (**Torre de los Lujanes**) once a prison for Francis I of France, who struggled with Charles V for control of Italy but was captured at the Battle of Pavía in 1525. Also in the Square is the **Casa de Cisneros**, family home of the Cardinal who was one of the most powerful of Isabella's supporters and advisers.

Continuing along Calle Mayor you come to the huge cathedral of **Nuestra Señora de Almudena**, a pretentious and ugly 19th-century work which lies to the south of the Royal Palace (Palacio Real). The street that runs along the east side of the Palace is the Calle Bailén which runs south as far as the (**Plaza de San Francisco**) Square of St Francis. Here above a slope which runs down to the Rio Manzanares is the largest church in Madrid, **San Francisco el Grande** built in the 18th century in Rénaissance style, on a circular plan above which rises a dome with two towers and a lantern. The interior is vast and remote, though an early work by Goya in the Bernardino chapel adds interest to a visit and there are also paintings by Ribera and Zurbáran.

The Royal Palace (**Palacio Nacional or Palacio del Oriente**), at the northern end of Calle Bailén, is set in vast grounds which stretch down to the Manzanares River. It was built for the first Bourbon King, Philip V, by the Italian architects Juvara (who built some of Turin), Sachetti and Ventura Rodriguez. The palace is built round a central courtyard. Its southern, classical-style, facade faces a large court which stretches towards the cathedral of Nuestra Señora de la Almudena and its northern face looks out over formal gardens ending in an apex pointing towards the Plaza de España.

The interior, which may be visited on a guided tour, is in the grand style with a splending marble staircase by Sabatini and wall and ceiling paintings by Tiepolo, Mengs and Velasquez, among others. The main apartments open to the public are those of Charles III, furnished in the style of his period; the apartments of Maria Cristina of Hapsburg, mother of Alfonso XIII, which date from the latter part of the 19th century; and the private apartments of Alfonso XIII and his wife Victoria Eugenia, grand-daughter of Queen Victoria.

No expense was spared on these apartments in order to create an opulent setting for monarchs. Visiting them, you cannot help meditating on the grand illusion which swept Europe from the 16th century on, rallying populations around monarchs who were symbols of national power to be venerated and followed even if the individual holder of the throne was an imbecile or rogue. In the end, even the monarchs ceased to believe in their divine mission and many of the rulers of Europe, like Alfonso XIII, gave up their position to others who claimed to represent the people in a new and, sometimes, more democratic manner.

Nevertheless, there was a Golden Age of art, literature and learning in Europe during these centuries, and it touched Spain as much as anywhere else. Look at how Tiepolo portrays the power and majesty of the Spanish monarch in the small room called Saleta, avoiding in his airy way the implications of the subject. Look out also for his paintings in the Guard Room (**Salon de Alabanderos**) and the Throne Room (**Salon del Trono**) which is in the Charles III apartments. Here you will find the Goya portraits of Charles

IV, which are hardly flattering, but then Goya was a realist to whom pomp, ceremony, honour and glory meant little.

As well as furniture and paintings, the Royal Palace houses a superb collection of porcelain and a library occuping 24 rooms. For the warlike there is a Royal Armoury (**Armería Real**) and for those interested in horse transport there is a splendid Coach Museum **Caballerizas** in the Campo de Moro in the northern grounds of the palace.

Around the Grand Via

The Grand Via, officially called Avenida Jose Antonio after the founder of the Falange who was one of Franco's heroes, forms the northern side of a triangle whose other sides are the Calle de Bailén and Calle Mayor and, at its continuation east of the Puerta del Sol, the Calle de Alcalá. Within this triangle and along the Gran Via lies the business and social centre of Madrid with shops, offices, banks, cinemas, hotels and restaurants ensuring a constant flow of people and traffic.

At its western end the Gran Vía starts its life at the **Plaza de España** in the centre of which the doleful figure of Don Quixote and the rotund Sancho Panza stand before their creator, Cervantes, all cast in bronze. On the north-western corner of the Plaza rise two skyscrapers, the **Torre de Madrid** and **Edificio España**, symbols of the new Spain. At its eastern end the Gran Vía joins the Calle de Alcalá which goes on to the **Plaza de la Cibeles** where the Greek Goddess of fertility splashes through a fountain in her chariot, while the Madrid traffic circulates round her to the shrill whistles of the traffic police.

There are several points of interest around the Gran Vía. By the palace is the **Plaza Oriente**, a creation of Joseph Bonaparte who had it decorated with 47 statues of kings of Spain from the time of the Visigoths to his day. On its east side is the Opera House **Teatro Real del Opera** which was opened in 1850 and has been host to most major opera singers since then. The Plaza Isabel II lies to the west and further along is the Square of the Barefoot Carmelites **Plaza de las Descalzadas** named for the convent here **the Convento**

de las Descalzas Reales, which, despite its name, became the most luxurious haven of retreat from the world for the noble families of Spain. The convent is a treasure house of paintings, tapestries, holy relics and other works of art bequeathed by grateful noble ladies, including Juana of Austria, daughter of Charles V. Nearby to the south along the Calle del Arenal, is the **Church of San Ginés** which contains some El Greco paintings including 'Christ driving the money changers from the Temple'.

The Gran Vía is, of course, the place to see and to be seen. Most of Madrid's population seems to be there at one time or another, especially in the evening between 7pm and 10pm when the whole of Spain goes out for the evening paseo (stroll) before dinner which is eaten at 10 pm or even later.

The Gran Vía is popular because you can window shop, sit in a café or simply stroll around. It is centrally situated for both rich and poor, unlike the Paseo de la Castellana which has smart cafés but is in the north-east corner of Madrid in a predominantly middle-class quarter. The Gran Vía is for everyone and it is the best place for a visitor to sit and watch Madrileños during that significant time of day between the end of work and the evening meal.

The smart east side of Madrid

The eastern edge of central Madrid is traversed by a handsome tree lined boulevard of splendid proportions bordered by well to do mansions. This boulevard has several changes of name as it progresses from its southern end at the Atocha station to the northern extremity where modern government buildings and the Museum of Natural Sciences (**Museo de Ciencias Naturales**) and the Council for Scientific Research (**Consejo Superior de Investigaciones Cientificas**) are situated near the Plaza San Juan de la Cruz. From Atocha to the Plaza de Cibeles and its magnificent fountain the boulevard is called the Paseo del Prado and in its vicinity are many of the great museums of Madrid and the new cultural centre named after Queen Sofia.

At its southern end the Paseo goes along the Botanical Gardens (**Jardines Botánicos**) where Charles III of Spain, a keen naturalist, spent many hours in the study of botany and medicinal plants. The gardens are a delight to stroll in and the street along their southern edge, Calle Claudio Moyana, is ideal for people who like to browse among books for it has a permanent book fair. The large building across the street from the gardens is, appropriately enough the Ministry of Agriculture.

As you stroll north along the Paseo del Prado you pass the great **Prado Museum**, with which we have dealt in a special section. Opposite to it, perhaps a little incongruously, since the priceless collections of the Prado are the product of an age of privilege minorities, is the house of the Workers syndicates or Trade Unions.

Behind the Prado are a number of interesting buildings which you pass on the way west to the vast Park of El Retiro. Immediately behind the Prado is the Church of St Gerome **(San Jerónimo Reales)** and next to it the Academy of the Spanish Language **(Academia de la Lengua)** which watches over the purity of Spanish and is the authority in all linguistic questions.

Nearby along the Calle de la Lealtad is the **Cason del Buen Retiro** which contains works of 19th century artists and the Picasso painting 'Guerniea' which he painted in protest against the bombing of the undefended Basque village and which has only recently returned to Spain. Across the square is the Army Museum **(Museo del Ejército)** with its two tall towers. The Museum was founded by Manuel Godoy minister to Charles IV and contains uniforms and weapons of the Spanish army since its earliest years.

The western end of the Calle de la Libertad comes into the Plaza de Canovas del Castillo which has an attractive 18th century Neptune fountain. If you cross the Plaza you come to the Carrera de San Jerónimo and the centre of political life, a small unassuming building where the Spanish parliament **(Cortes Españolas)**, also called Congreso de los Diputados sits.

The Cortes have governed Spanish life since feudal times when they represented the interests of the different regions of Spain and of their lords. Even the most autocratic monarchs have had to engage the support of the Cortes to carry out their plans as Charles V did when he wanted to establish his position as ruler of Spain though the true heir, his mother, was still alive.

Under the Bourbons the Cortes were first abolished and then corrupted. They were unable to exert their influence over the country at a time of national crisis and during the 19th century lost the power to maintain national unity. Under Franco the Cortes were reduced to an assembly of 'yes men' but with the end of his dictatorship there has been a renaissance of their national role. A mark of their new democratic status and of the support they have from present day Spanish society was seen in 1981 when a misguided Colonel Tejero of the Civil Guard thought that it would be possible to hold the country to ransom by a show of force and led an assault on the Cortes, holding its members hostage for 24 hours. His high handed action produced a mass reaction in the streets of Madrid. The appeal of King Juan Carlos to the people and especially to the army brought to a speedy end an incident which will live on as a ridiculous, though historic, moment in the history of the Spanish people.

Continuing along the Paseo del Prado you come to a delightful little semicircle of green, the **Plaza de la Lealtad**, with a fountain in the midst of which is a column which commemorates the national uprising against the Napoleonic troops. This was savagely put down, but precipitated the Peninsular War which in Spain is known as the War of Independence (**Guerra de la Independencia**).

The large building overlooking the square is the Stock Exchange (**La Bolsa**) for in this quarter business and art mix amicably together. Further along the Paseo is the vast building of the Bank of Spain (**Banco de España**) which looks across the Plaza de la Cibeles, and the chariot of the goddess in her foaming fountain, to the palatial Post Office (**Correos y Telegrafos**).

Beyond the Plaza de la Cibeles the great boulevard becomes the Paseo de Recoletos which stretches as far as Columbus Square (**Plaza de Colon**) passing on the way the Archaeological Museum (**Museo Arqueologico**) where you can enjoy the reproduction of the caves of Altamira as the originals are now closed to the public, except by special request.

The quarter to the east of the Paseo de Recoletos, and its continuation the Paseo de la Castellana, has become one of the most fashionable and affluent of Madrid and its main artery the Calle de Serrano which runs parallel to the grand Paseos, from the Puerte de Alcalá arch of triumph, is as elegant as that of any capital city with banks, and embassies, high fashion boutiques, restaurants as well as expensive apartment blocks. It also has a superb 300 room collection of paintings and works of art at the **Museo Lázaro Galdiano** which was bequeathed to the city by its collector Señor Gadiano who died in 1948.

The most superb feature of east Madrid owes as much to nature as to human endeavour and this is the **Jardínes del Retiro**. The 130 hectares (321 acres) of land which contain woods, formal gardens, temples, and other buildings, statues and ponds including the huge El Estanque where a 19th century monument to Alfonso XII rises above the trees. Once a royal estate created by Philip IV the Jardínes del Retiro are a Madrileño playground where at weekends there is a wonderful cross section of Madrid life from the average well turned out bourgeois citizens with their immaculately dressed children, who show every sign of undoing their parents' handiwork, to the rebellious adolescents sporting provocative hair styles and T shirts. The poor, the rich, the young and the old all pass before you in this pleasure garden. On the Estanque boats glide to and fro loaded with families or floating high in the water with only a pair of lovers. The scene is reminiscent of those idyllic images painted by the Impressionists in which everyone is cocooned in a world of sun dappled happiness. You cannot help daydreaming as you sit watching the crowds go by that in Spain perhaps this world still lingers on.

☆ ☆ ☆ ☆ ☆

The Prado

The greatest of all the Museums of Madrid, and by itself a good reason for visiting Madrid, is the **Museo del Prado** which opened to the public in 1819. The idea of getting together some of the private collections of the monarchy and the nobility may have been Joseph Bonaparte's, but it was put into effect by Fernando VII. He gathered together the collections in a building which was originally intended as a natural history museum. The unique quality of the Prado collection is that most of it was amassed privately by the kings of the Golden Age of Spain: Charles V, Philip II, and Philip IV. It presents as a whole an illuminating insight into the life, thoughts and ideas of their times from the grand and idealised view provided by the painters of court life and church to the horror-struck visions of Goya.

The work of the Spanish painters as well as those of Dutch and Italian painters bought on the advice of Rubens and Velasquez reveal something of the taste and beliefs of the monarchs, churchmen and their courts. In this brief survey of this treasure house we are focusing on those paintings which reflect some of the personalities and events of Spanish history.

Among the Italian pictures is a splendid and truthful equestrian portrait of **Charles V** by Titian. The little king in his war-like attire is mounted on a black charger and is apparently eager to go into battle, though his body, motionless and remote, suggests someone far removed from the actuality of life and inhabiting the cloistered world of people with complete power. Less objective, perhaps, and more designed to please his royal patron, are Titian's epic pictures entitled **Philip II after the battle of Lepanto commending his son to God**, the propagandist painting **The Church Upheld by Spain**, and the portrait of the young **Charles V**, painted when he visited Bologna and which pleased the Emperor so much that he made Titian a count of the Lateran Palace. The painting was later given to Charles I of England but was returned to Spain after the King's execution. Another significant Titian painting is the one entitled **The Glory**, which was specially commissioned. In this Charles V is shown without his imperial robes and is kneeling with his wife, Elizabeth of

Portugal, his son (later Philip II) and other members of his family. This is one of the paintings he took with him when he retired to the Monastery at Yuste.

Since Charles V was Emperor of the vast Hapsburgs dominions, the Prado paintings connected with him have a broader, more European base than those which were collected after his abdication when the Hapsburg dominions of the east were separated from the Spanish inheritance of Philip II. In the early years of the Golden Age of Spain most of the paintings that decorated palaces and noble homes came from Italy or the Netherlands and dealt with the subjects popular there: classical themes, landscapes etc. The character and tastes of the Spanish patrons of the national artists soon brought about a change and you will find a considerable increase in religious paintings portraying realistically the lives of saints or biblical incidents. By the 17th century nearly half of all paintings produced by Spanish artists were of this kind, and most artists were embracing religious themes.

The Golden Age of Spanish painting may be said to have begun in the reign of Philip III. This was marked by the births of Velasquez in Seville in 1599, **Zurbarán**, in Fuente de Cantos, Badajoz in 1598, **Murillo**, also in Seville in 1617, and **Ribera** in Játiva, Valencia in 1591, at the end of the reign of Philip II. There were, of course, many followers of the masters as well as minor painters working in this period, all of whom are represented in the Prado.

The artistic flowering of all these masters happened during the reign of Philip IV, a keen supporter of the arts. Philip appreciated early on that Diego de Silva Velásquez was a young man of unusual talents and enrolled him as a court painter. He was rewarded by being made the subject of the greatest series of portraits of a monarch ever made. Velasquez's paintings of Philip IV range from the pink-cheeked young man in a full-length portrait of 1628 to the mirror image of the king in the wonderful painting **Las Meninas** so called because it shows Velasquez at work painting the Princess Margarita with two dwarf attendants, and other shadowy background members of the court while, in a small mirror, there appears Philip IV and his wife paying a surprise visit to the artist's studio. This is one of those superb and perfect works like Giovanni Bellini's **Storm**, or Piero della Francesca's **Nativity**, which are beyond words and it alone is worth a trip to Madrid. Unfortunately, many people agree and so you have to get to the Prado early in the day or off-season to avoid the crowds.

Other royal pictures by Velásquez in the Prado include an equestrian portrait of Philip IV, whose early moustaches became more and more sprightly with each succeeding portrait, and a portrait of Philip's wife, Isabel of France, who was the daughter of Mariá de Medici and Henry IV of Navarre; the debonair and astute king who brought France peace after the dreadful religious wars of the Catholics and Huguenots. There is also a portrait of Margaret of Austria, Philip's daughter, though Juan Bautista del Mazo, Velásquez's son-in-law, may have had a hand in painting this one. Most charming of all the royal portraits is that of Prince Balthasar Carlos who is seen as a young boy hunting and, unforgettably, riding a rotund little pony that seems about to burst at the seams. According to legend, the pony died before the painting was finished and was stuffed for the final sittings.

Velásquez also painted one grand political set piece. Entitled **The Surrender at Breda** and commemorating a Spanish victory over Justinus of Nassau. This depicts the Spanish commander, Spinola, placing his hand in a kindly gesture on his opponent's shoulder before the assembled armies, behind which rise a forest of lances. Unlike so many paintings of historic events this is a masterpiece.

A most prolific painter, Velásquez found time to paint the minions of the palace, the dwarfs, buffoons and servants and these have a tenderness and compassion that to my mind outstrips the emotional content of most religious paintings. Another realist was Francesco Zurbarán, whose gallery of monks and friars shows them as people unlike the etherealized madonnas of Murillo's Immaculate conceptions.

Also, well represented among Spanish painters in the Prado is **Ribera**, known as l'Espagnolo, who worked much of his life in Italy, where he developed his Caravaggesque style of painting.

An oddball in the world of Spanish painters whose work was not highly regarded until the 20th century is **Domenico Theotocopolous**, better known as **El Greco**. The Greek was born in Crete in 1541 and arrived in Spain in 1576 during the reign of Philip II who commissioned work from him but did not like the result. Others did, however, including Don Juan de Silva, Knight of Santiago, who is believed to be the subject of the notable portrait called The Man with a Hand on his Breast (**Caballero de la mano al pecho**). More typical of El Greco's fevered style is **The Adoration of the Shepherds** and **The Resurrection**, where the elongated Mannerist figures writhe anxiously about the canvas expressing, perhaps, the neuroticism of a period when the Inquisition was feared by all as much as any present-day secret police.

Last of the great painters of Spain before the moderns is **Goya** who lived during the reign of Charles III and Charles IV. Goya was born in Fuendetodos, Zaragoza, in 1746, and began to work on tapestries for the royal factory in Madrid in the 1770s. The utterly captivating and light-hearted designs for these are kept together in one room in the Prado. Goya's cartoons for the tapestries were, in fact, oil paintings – which annoyed the tapestry makers who were used to working from cartoons designed with the limited range of tapestry colours in mind.

Between the tapestry paintings and the Black paintings of the **Horrors of War** and the moralising cartoons, called **Capricios**, also kept together in one room, lies

Goya's life and the whole range of his work including the royal portraits of around 1800. The largest of these is the family group which shows Charles IV with his wife, Maria Luisa of Parma and other members of the family, including the Crown Prince, Fernando, later to be King and then prisoner of Napoleon. Charles IV was an ineffective monarch much under the influence of his prime minister Manuel de Godoy, reputed to have been the lover of the Queen and in any event a friend of Napoleon, who allowed the French troops into Spain. The unflattering royal portrait seems to reflect Goya's private feelings about the King and Queen.

The most notorious of all Goya's paintings is the **Maja Desnuda**, which makes a pair with the **Maja Vestida**. According to legend, both the naked and dressed lady on the settee, whose head seems not to belong to the body, is the Duchess of Alba, a friend and patron of Goya. The truth of this only the Duchess and Goya could confirm.

Of all the Spanish painters so superbly presented at the Prado none exhibits the variety of emotions, themes, and styles that Goya shows. To examine his work alone would take weeks, an impossible assignment for a visitor faced with a collection of paintings which includes masterpieces of the Italian, Dutch, German, French and English schools.

☆ ☆ ☆ ☆ ☆

Madrid's west side

To the west of the Royal Palace the land slopes away towards the Manzanares river. These slopes were a battleground during the Civil War and much of the city in this area was destroyed. Today there are few signs of the bloody struggle except for the ruined barracks (**Cuartel de la Montaña**). It was here that the occupants were massacred in 1936 when the citizens of Madrid, aided by Asturian miners who blew up the walls, entered the barracks to collect arms for the defence of Madrid against Franco's troops.

Below the barracks stretches the peaceful and delightful park (**Parque del Oeste**) which looks over the river to the old hunting grounds of the kings of Spain (**Casa del Campo**) which are now a huge park in a corner of which is Madrid Zoo and an amusement park. Reached by cable car from the Paseo del Pintor Rosales above the Parque del Oeste. Midway along the Paseo de la Florida which runs along the lower edge of the park, is the church and pilgrimage place of all admirers of Francisco Goya y Lucientes, (**El Panteón de Goya**) (also **Ermita de San Antonio de la Florida**). Goya is buried in the church but the main reason for a visit is not to pay respect at his tomb but to enjoy the wonderful frescoes with which the painter decorated the church in 1798. Unlike most frescoes on church walls and ceilings these do not rely on flying angels and groups posed on cumulus clouds for effect but on Goya's masterly portrayal of the Madrid people. The cupola paintings with the people standing by or sitting on the balustrade along its lower edge is particularly enchanting.

To the north of the Parque del Oeste you will find several museums. The former home of the Marquess of Cerralba contains furniture, tapestries and armour, the Museo de America has a superb collection of Aztec and Peruvian art and artefacts and the modern art museum is a showplace for Spanish artists of the 20th century. Also, in this area which is on the edge of the University city is the Palacio de Moncloa, home of the Priiime Minister of Spain. The University city itself is relatively new and was re-erected after the old one was destroyed in the Civil War. It has little of special interest.

Royal palaces around Madrid

Many of the most interesting and historic towns of old Castile are near enough to Madrid for a day's trip to them from the capital, though this hardly allows time for a satisfactory visit. Also, within reach of Madrid are a number of palaces of historical interest, including the **Escorial**, from where Philip II ruled his vast empire for much of his reign.

The Escorial at San Lorenzo del Escorial in the Guadar-rama mountains combines a palace, church and monastery.

It was built by Philip II, whose initial idea was to construct a mausoleum for his father, Charles V. First Philip employed Juan Bautista de Toledo, who had worked in Rome, as architect. When he died, the king enrolled Juan de Herrera, Bautista's pupil.

Numerous theories about the design and character of the Escorial have been expounded. Some commentators suggest that its structure refers to the grid on which St Lawrence was martyred while others prefer the theory that its proportions were worked out by geomancy. However, the most likely reason for its design is that its character satisfied Philip II's sense of austerity and order. Philip was an intensely serious and humourless man profoundly aware of the responsibilities of his kingship which in his eyes included the reunification of the world under one Christian philosophy and the need to defend Spain against the powers that envied her good fortune in having discovered and taken possession most of the Americas.

It seems natural then, that Philip should have looked to Rome, the spiritual centre of the Christian world, for inspiration. However, Philip's Rome had nothing to do with the frivolities of papal or royal courts, and the Escorial had to represent Renaissance Rome stripped of all inessential decorations. The Escorial, to coin a term applied to modern architecture, was to be a machine to live in, and was designed to bring about a united Christian world. An absurd idea in retrospect, but not so different from creating Empires modelled on the home country. The result was the magnificent but coldly rational ensemble of buildings whose power still impresses today. The quadrilateral complex of buildings stands on the edge of the village looking out over the countryside in which olive trees and poplars grow. From a distance you would mistake it for a grand military barracks were it not for the towers and dome of the Temple (**Tempio**), the great church that dominates the whole vast complex of buildings.

Entrance to the church is from the King's Courtyard (**Patio del Rey**). The interior of the Greek cross structure is

impressive. Four huge columns soar up to the roof, supporting the cupola, and beyond is the high altar with its massive
reredos. To each side of the altar are groups of gilded bronze
statuary, one of Charles V and his family at prayer and the
other of Philip II and his wives, not including Mary Tudor.
The groups, created during the king's lifetime by Pompeo
and Leoni Leone, who were contemporaries of Benvenutto
Cellini are an impressive reminder of the domestic and public
life of the two powerful monarchs.

Below the Temple lies the Royal Pantheon (**Panteón de los
Reyes**) in which are buried nearly all the kings of Spain since
the time of Charles V. Philip V, one of the absentees, found
the place so gloomy he asked to be buried in the Bourbon
palace at La Granja near Segovia. Don Juan of Austria is
also nearby in the pantheon of the Princes along with all the
royal children who died in infancy and whose remains are
contained in an elaborate white marble tomb.

The palace is less macabre and, despite its reputation, not
a gloomy place. Ironically, it has helped to make the Escorial
more of a memorial to Philip II than to his father, as he had
intended. In the simple furnished rooms occupied by Philip,
in the **Libraries**, and the **New Museums** you receive an
impression of a house occupied by a scholarly, perhaps even
pedantic man, quite unlike the despotic autocrat of the
popular imagination.

As he grew older and his carefully laid plans failed, first
the Armada and then the revolt of the Netherlands, Philip
became more of a recluse surrounded by his private advisers.
When he became ill with a painful disease that caused him to
waste away with gangrene Philip lived in the rooms where he
had always worked and slept, and which are little changed
today. In them are a crucifix, a writing desk, and a bed by
which there is a skull with a golden crown which Philip
ordered when he knew he was fatally ill, perhaps to remind
him of the folly of human ambitions.

The Bourbons did not like the Escorial and did their best
to brighten it up. Their efforts are visible in the **Bourbon
apartments** where tapestries and Pompeian-style decorations
cover the walls, and in the **Hall of the Battles**, where murals

celebrate famous victories including the one at St Quentin against the French in thanks for which Philip vowed to build the Temple and monastery of San Lorenzo del Escorial.

Philip also had another palace at **El Pardo**, to the north of Madrid, but this was burned down in 1604 and rebuilt by Philip III. The contrast of this largely Bourbon-decorated palace with El Escorial sums up the difference between the two regimes. El Pardo reflects the rococo French palaces of Louis XV and XVI, with their elegant furniture, gilded plaster work and silk hangings. This is the world of Fragonard and Fêtes Champêtres, of a court given over to social life and living for the day. Luxury is the keynote of the **objets d'art**, the chandeliers, marble busts, clocks, Sèvres porcelain and the fine tapestries from Brussels and the Royal Tapestry Factory (**Real Fabric a de Tapices**) are the finest in the land.

In the grounds of the Palace El Pardo is a pavilion which, like the Cottage of the Prince (**Casita del Principe**) at the Escorial was built specially for Charles IV and sums up perfectly the pleasure-living world of the Bourbons.

The Bourbon world is seen at its most opulent at **La Granja de San Ildefonso** to the south of Segovia. The original hunting lodge and then monastery were converted by the orders of Philip V who was also Duke of Anjou, into a palace comparable to the chateaux of the Loire by the Italian architects Sacchetti and Juvara.

The main building, in French Renaissance style, has two major courtyards, the Coach Court (**Patio de los Coches**) and the Horseshoe Court (**Patio de las Herraduras**). Behind the buildings rises the church, with its dome and lantern, in which Philip V and his wife are buried.

Though attractive enough for anyone not surfeited with Bourbon architecture, the palace is not as good a reason for visiting San Ildefonso as the gardens, which are delightful. Designed in the style of Le Nôtre, who landscaped Versailles, they cover 360 acres and contain 26 large fountains as well as many smaller ones. There is also a lake so vast as to be named the sea (**El Mar**).

La Granja did not satisfy Philip V's enthusiasm for

palaces, however, for to the south of Madrid at **Aranjuez** is yet another of his efforts to imitate the glory of Versailles. This one even has its own Trianon, the Farmer's House (**Casita del Labrador**) with a courtyard adorned with statues and a fountain and surrounded by a building with elegant rooms which few farmers could have imagined even in their wildest dreams but which satisfied the Rousseauesque fantasies of the 18th-century royal courts.

Chapter Five:
Land of Don Quixote and The Conquistadors

The part of Spain between the central cordilleras and the mountains of what was once the Roman province of Baética and is now Andalucía was the territory disputed between the Christian kingdoms of Castile and Leon and Aragon and the Moors. Although it shares some of the same historic background as Old Castile, you will find less evidence here of the long-drawn-out struggle in fortified cities and hill-top castles.

The nature of land south of the capital cities of Toledo and Madrid has much to do with this. It is dry and inhospitable. Even today it is almost unpopulated, especially in the area between Toledo and Córdoba and west to Extremadura.

To the east of Madrid, however, on the borders of Castile and what was the kindgom of Aragon when at its greatest extent, you will find remains of many great feudal fiefs with their towns and fortified castles. In La Mancha there are other features which make a journey worthwhile. This is the land of Don Quixote where old windmills rise out of the flat landscape and deserted castles stand like sentinels in what was once the outpost of Christian Spain. There is little moisture here, certainly not enough for irrigation, though reservoirs are being created along the Tagus and Guadiana rivers to encourage agricultural development. Until now crops have been raised on the principle of allowing them to survive without irrigation, a system known as **secano.** In this way olives and vineyards which require little water are grown and there is a wine industry (see The Wines of Spain, page 20). Sheep raising, once the most important activity of the region and one which enriched the lords of the **meseta,** is carried on still.

111

To the west of New Castile lies Extremadura, so-named because it was once considered a far-away place beyond the Duoro River and one with little potential. Perhaps the rigours of life there explain why so many of the early adventurers who went to explore the Americas came from this region.

The borders of Aragon

The north-east corner of New Castile has a special importance for it was the border with the rival kingdom of Aragon which, even after the union of Ferdinand and Isabella, maintained its own identity. Along this part of New Castile the feudal lords established their towns and built castles, most which are still there today. It is a fascinating part of Spain to explore.

The farthest north of these border towns is **Siguenza,** a town which rises spectacularly in tiers of red-tiled houses above the River Henares. The old town clusters round the 12th-century castle, now the Parador Nacional Castillo de Siguenza, and the Cathedral. As in Avila, the Cathedral appears to be part of the defences of the town even looking like a fortress. Its interior is more churchlike, with a mixture of Romanesque and Gothic styles with Plateresque additions. There are some good carvings and the paintings include a Titian and an El Greco. The main point of interest, however, is the tomb of El Doncel de Siguenza, who was a page boy called Martin de Arce. He was a member of Isabella's retinue and was killed at the gates of Granada. According to legend, the Queen was so touched by his death that she commissioned a statue of him for his tomb. The result is there for you to see in the touching image of a medieval young man lying, book in hand, in the chapel of the Arce family.

Outside the Cathedral is a most attractive colonnaded Plaza Mayor, a Renaissance-style Town Hall. To the east of Siguenza lies **Molina de Aragon,** a town whose castle has been reduced to crumbling ruins, though its five towers still evoke the days of feudal rivalries and marauding armed bands; and to the west is **Guadalajara.** Today an industrial satellite of Madrid, in the days of the Catholic Monarchs Guadalajara was the territory of the powerful Mendoza family whose most famous figure was Cardinal Mendoza, an appointee of the Borgia Pope who became adviser to Ferdinand and Isabella. From his time there remains the Palace of the Duke of Infantado, a magnificent building with a colonnaded facade and fine interior courtyard. Francis I of France was kept prisoner here after his failed attempt to challenge the Spanish domination of Milan and his capture at the Battle of Pavia; Philip II's marriage to Elisabeth of Valois also took place in the palace's vast halls.

South-east of **Guadalajara** lies the vast reservoir known as the Sea of Castile (**Mar de Castilla**), an artificial lake into which the young Tagus flows through rocky gorges. The lake is intended to improve the agricultural possibilities of the land below the mountainous region of the Alcarria.

Another range of mountains in this region, the Serranía de Cuenca, extends south-east to the town of **Cuenca** on the River Júcar. The town overlooks the river, apparently suspended over the cliffs with its houses protruding over the cliff face, a view best seen from the walk along the river. Behind the cliff-edge houses is the Cathedral, a Gothic building with Renaissance decorations. Its treasury shares the role of Cuenca Art Centre and Diocesan Museum, which boasts two El Grecos. There is also, perhaps surprisingly in this ancient and remote town, a museum of Spanish abstract art in one of the hanging houses (**casas colgadas**). There are some dizzy views of the surrounding landscape through the windows which many visitors find as much, or sometimes more, interesting than the contents of the museum.

The Júcar river which protects the cliffs of Cuenca does a similar service for **Alarcón,** though this town is less spectacularly sited on a small hill. The castle here stands on the edge of the river's ravine. It was once owned by the Marquess of Villena, a feudal lord who at first resented the interference of Ferdinand and Isabella in his kingdom but later became, at times, their ally. The waters of the Júcar, controlled nowadays by a dammed up river, once presented a serious obstacle to enemies. Villena also owned the castle at

113

Belmonte, to the east, but it was abandoned and became derelict until restored by Eugenia de Montijo in the 19th century.

This part of New Castile is in Don Quixote country and Mota del Cuervo, where the sad-faced knight attacked the windmills under the impression that they were giants, is only 15 km (10 miles) away from Belmonte.

The story of Don Quixote and his loyal squire, Sancho Panza, was written by Miguel de Cervantes Saavedra, who was born at Alcalá de Henares near Madrid in 1547. After an adventurous youth which included action at the Battle of Lepanto and captivity by Algerian corsairs, he devoted himself to writing. Don Quixote was a satire on the noble Spanish society of the 17th century which had become rigid and decadent. The noble knight Don Quixote sets off with the best of intentions but somehow always ends up in absurd situations owing to his inability to distinguish between his delusions and reality. At one time he attacks a flock of sheep which he takes for an enemy army and at another he charges a windmill thinking it is a giant. The reality for Spain during Cervantes' lifetime was that after the reigns of Charles V and Philip II the country was impoverished and its hierarchical society was incapable of reacting to the political situation of 17th and 18th century Europe.

The choice of La Mancha as the land of Don Quixote seemed an appropriate one to Cervantes for here was a waste land in which ruined castles spoke of times past and of noble ambitions that had turned to dust. Today, though the land is still arid, there are over a million acres of vineyards in La Mancha, making it the largest single wine-producing area in Spain. Among the best known wines of the region which produce over 5 million gallons of mostly white wine, are those of Manzanares and Valdepeñas. The dry soil also produces olives and some cereals.

To the east of these wine regions, which are to be found on the E25 road from Madrid to Granada, is **Ciudad Real** which became royal in 1420 when the kings of Spain began to establish their authority among the powerful knights of the orders of Calatrava who lived on the borders of the Moorish

Kingdom of Andalucia. This was an area of continual struggle between Christians and Moors until the 17th century when the last remnants of the infidel occupation were erased.

Though the capital of La Mancha for a brief period, Ciudad Real, which has a cathedral and preserves a gateway of its 14th-century town walls, was always far outshone by Toledo to the north.

Toledo

More than any other city in Spain, **Toledo** encapsulates all the kaleidoscopic ingredients of Spanish history. Its location in the centre of the Iberian peninsula, the island character of its rocky crag, wrapped in the horseshoe curve of the River Tagus, and its antiquity all conspired to make it the true centre of Spain until Philip II decided to move the capital to Madrid.

The Romans fortified and built the first city on the site of Toledo, though little remains of their work except for a few ruins to the north where an arena once entertained the soldiers of the garrison of Toletum. The Visigoths made the city their capital, but used the Roman buildings as quarries for materials for their own town, later abandoning it to the Moors who were arriving in an unstoppable tide from the south. From the 8th to the 11th century Toledo was part of the Emirate of Cordoba and capital of an independent Moorish Kingdom. Thus, by the time Alfonso XI arrived with the armies of the Reconquest in 1085 the population of Toledo was very mixed indeed, containing descendants of the Romans, Goths, Moors and large numbers of Jews who had arrived as traders as far back as Roman times.

Until 1391 all the various races lived peacefully together in Toledo, as, indeed, in many parts of Spain. The Jews were valued for their business and administrative ability and the Moors for their learning and craftsmanship. The fervour of the Reconquest of Spain changed the situation, however. As in similar circumstances before, and since, the leaders of the drive to unify the country needed to abolish all rival claims to the loyalties of the inhabitants. If you were not with the Reconquest it was assumed you were against it. To be with the Reconquest meant embracing all its principles: an unquestioning dedication to Spain, to the Catholic church and to its leaders. Thousands upon thousands paid lip service to the new conditions of life but remained still suspect, especially when it was discovered that they practised their deeply held faiths in secret.

Thus began the massacres of Jews and Moors that were to blacken Spain's record. The first of these was in 1391, in the reign of Henry of Trastamara, when the entire congregation at the **Toledo Synagogue** was massacred by Christians fired by the evangelical spirt of Vincent Ferrer, a Dominican with an English father and a Spanish mother and who was a noted rabble rouser. He was later canonised. The Moors fared a little better for a while and continued to improve Toledo with their work, which can still be seen today in churches, synagogues, and private houses. Most notable is their work in the chapter house of the cathedral, the El Tránsito Synagogue and the Church of St James outside the walls. With the arrival of Ferdinand and Isabella the crusade against all those who did not completely share the new ideals of a united Catholic Spain was intensified, the Moors were expelled and more massacres took place. There were conversions, too, with Archbishop Cisneros, the **eminence grise** of the Ferdinand and Isabella court, converting some 40,000 Toledans to the True Faith.

Most of the Toledo you see today bears some sign of the city's intense past. Indeed the town has been carefully preserved so that many visitors think of Toledo as a great museum of Spanish history.

There are two ways into the town across the river: over the bridge on the 14th-century Puerta San Martino at the eastern side of the town, or over the Alcantara Bridge under the Castillo de S. Servando. The main inland gate in the city walls was once the Puerta Antigua de Bisagra, which the Moors built and through which Alfonso VI and El Cid made their entry in 1085. However, today you enter by the Puerta Nueva de Bisagra, through which the Madrid road passes. This impressive gateway lies on the north side of the city and beyond it, outside the walls, are the remains in a public garden, of the Roman arena, as well as a school and museum, the Hospital de Tavera. The original hospital, built by Cardinal Tavera, has some interesting pictures in the museum section, notably the Emperor Charles V by Titian and a Holy Family by El Greco.

Once through the Puerta de Bisagra, you are in an inner city whose perimeter is marked by by the Puerta de Sol, a large double-arched construction in the Mudéjar style. There is a good view of the city to be had from the gate: ask the carctaker's permission to go up.

Following the curving street called Venancio Gonzalez, you reach the Zocodover, a busy square where tourists are set down from their excursion coaches and the shops and cafés do a brisk trade. The name Zocodover is derived from the Arab 'Socco', or souk and a market is still held in the square one day a week.

Leaving the Zocodover by the Calle Comercio, you arrive eventually at Plaza de San Vicente where the church has interesting Mudéjar work on its exterior. Further on is San Clemente, with doorways finely carved in Plateresque style. A former church, San Roman is next door, its Mudéjar tower a distinctive landmark. San Roman now houses the **Museo de los Concilios y de la Cultura Visigoda,** a museum which preserves many relics from the Visigoth occupation, including frescoes and jcwellery.

From the Plaza San Vicente a narrow street (**Nuncio Viejo**) leads down to the **Cathedral.** The main (west) entrance faces the Town Hall square (**Plaza del Ayuntamiento**) on which are situated the **Town Hall** designed by El Greco's son, the Law Courts (**Audiencia**) and the **Archbishop's Palace (Palacio Arzobispale).** The cathedral front is impressive with its three great portals named from left to right Hell (**Puerta del Infierno**) Pardon (**Puerta del Perdon**) and Judgement (**Puerta del Juicio**). The elaborate 300ft tower rising by the cathedral is superb and the sound of its bells (the largest weighs 17 tons) unforgettable. The north door, the original entrance, named after the clock (**Puerta del Reloj**) and the south door with its lions (**Puerta de los Leones**) are also worth a visit.

If you have already visited some of the dark interiors of

117

other Spanish churches the interior of Toledo Cathedral comes as a joyful surprise. The abundance of stained glass windows lights up the tall interior whose nave and aisles lead up to the central choir which is bordered by chapels. If you walk past a tall wrought iron grille through the sanctuary you will find the high altar and huge carved polychrome reredos. In the sanctuary are various tombs of Castilian Kings but the most notable is that of Cardinal Mendoza, the powerful adviser of Ferdinand and Isabella. The whole area of the high altar is illuminated by light from the sky which enters through an opening in the vault which is disguised, or perhaps more correctly made more noticeable, by baroque decorations by Nariso Tomé and his family of sculptor sons. This is known as the Transparente.

There are many chapels and much statuary in Toledo Cathedral and of special interest is the Mozarabic chapel (**Capilla Mozárabe**) built on the orders of Cardinal Cisneiros, another powerful adviser of the Catholic monarchs. The peculiarity of this chapel is that the liturgy followed today is the same as that of the Christians who lived under Moorish rule.

From the Plaza del Ayuntamiento the street of El Salvador takes you to the church of San Tomé. Here you will find El Greco's most famous painting '**The Burial of the Count of Orgaz**', probably the most visited work of art in Toledo. If you find the crowds gaping at the picture a little oppressive then you can escape to the more tranquil atmosphere of El Greco's house at nearby Calle Samuel Levi. He lived here for most of his life and it now holds a small exhibition of his works.

Nearby in Paseo del Tránsito is one of the remaining synagogues of Toledo. This one was built by Samuel Levi, after whom the adjoining street is named, who was a financial adviser to Peter I of Castile. Continuing down Calle Samuel Levi you reach some viewpoints over the River Tagus and then turning up the street, of the Catholic Monarchs (**Calle Reyes Catolicos**) you come to the splendid monastery of St John of the Kings (**Monasterio de San Juan de Los Reyes**). This was commissioned by Ferdinand and

Isabella after the victory at Toro over the Portuguese supporters of La Betraneja. The fine church of the monastery has a Flemish/Spanish style and Mudéjar work in its interior.

On the western slopes of the crag on which Toledo is built is the Alcázar, a modern re-creation of the fortress in which the legendary Franco General Moscardo was besieged during the Civil War and refused to surrender though threatened with the death of his son who was a hostage held by the Republicans. Today the story is believed by some to be one of those morale inspiring inventions of war time.

Nearby to the north of the Alcázar is the handsome building commissioned by Cardinal Mendoza as a hospital. Today it is a museum which contains no less than 18 El Grecos. From this part of Toledo there is a view of the Alcantara bridge with its 13th century Mudéjar tower and of the Castle of San Servando on the other side of the River Tagus.

Aranjuez

To the east of Toledo lies **Aranjuez,** a green oasis in the arid Castilian plain, used by Ferdinand and Isabella and Charles V as a quiet retreat from cares of state in Madrid. The town has wide, tree-filled boulevards and shady squares. These together with its cool streets of 18th and 19th century buildings give it an attractive old-world atmosphere. The Bourbon kings established a residence here in a classical-style palace which is one of the show places of Aranjuez today. Its interior evokes the stylish, decadent days of the 19th century monarchy.

It was here, in 1808, that the incompetent Charles IV gathered his court in preparation for an escape from Napoleon's troops. Napoleon had gained free passage through Spain thanks to the machinations of Charles' minister, Manuel de Godoy, Duke of Alcudia, who not only had complete influence over the king but was also, it was said, the Queen's lover.

Godoy's sympathy for Napoleon was not shared by the people of Spain, who rebelled against his schemes, attacking

119

his house in Aranjuez. Charles was forced to abdicate in favour of his son Ferdinand, but Napoleon had other ideas and placed his brother, Joseph, on the Spanish throne. In so doing, he lit the fuse of a Spanish revolt, brilliantly but horrifyingly portrayed in Goya's 'Horrors of War' series, and given a direction and ultimate victory by Wellington in his masterly Peninsular campaign.

Extremadura – land of the warriors

Though to translate the name of this isolated land of plains and deep-cut river valleys as 'Extreme toughness' would not be inappropriate, the origin of Extremadura derives from the fact that it was the land beyond, that is to the south of, the River Duero. Though watered by two of Spain's major rivers, the Tagus and Guadiana, Extremadura is a dry arid land. To the west the mountains of Portugal absorb the Atlantic moisture and to the east stretches the dry plateau of New Castile.

For those who live in Extremadura life has always been hard, with little work except the tending of cattle and sheep and caring for the cork and olive groves. The young people have tended to seek their fortunes elsewhere. It is a land which had bred tough soldiers, inured equally to the freezing cold of winter and the burning sun of summer, impassive to the meagre rations and unquestioning endurance. It is the birth place of the Conquistadors who discovered and fought for the Spanish New World.

The similarity between the plateaus of Extremadura and the cattle-raising plains of Spanish America are remarkable. It is as if this impoverished and neglected corner of pre-Conquest Spain was the predestined prototype for the cattle-raising plains of Mexico, the Pampas of Argentina and the ranch lands of all central and South America.

The vast arid plateaus broken by dry sierras through which time and weather has carved deep ravines evoke the equivalent American plains as seen in a thousand movie Westerns. The men who ride the rangers are familiar, too, with their flat-topped black hats, trim waistcoats and close-fitting trousers. As in most dry lands, only the riverbeds

120

support permanent vegetation, with poplars growing tall among the evergreens. Most of the population lives in simple houses along the rivers that provide water for their crops, which include maize, wheat, tobacco and market garden produce. In the Tierra de Barros on the southern slopes of the Guadiana River valley the rich soil also supports vineyards and large wheatfields. The local industries include meat packing and the manufacture of dried sausages (chorizos), the most famous of which are those from the Montanchez area, between Cáceres and Medina.

Extremadura is also a land of legends and mysticism, especially in its northern half where demons were supposed to dwell in the uninhabited region called Las Hurdes, south of Ciudad Rodrigo. A more beneficent influence is the presence of the Virgin of **Guadalupe** at the eastern side of Extremadura between the Tagus and Guadiana. The dark-faced effigy of the Virgin was found by a cowherd in 1300 shortly before King Alfonso XI of Castile's victory over the Moors at the Battle of Salado. This notable event, which occurred 150 years before Ferdinand and Isabella began their final drive against the Moors, gave the Virgin a reputation for miraculous powers. She became patron of all the saints of Spain and the most powerful of all the patron saints of the New World.

Her shrine was a major centre of religious and commercial activity right up to the 16th and 17th centuries and was even visited by Christopher Columbus as well as most of the Conquistadors. The former arrived with a candle weighing about 3 kilos to thank her for saving him and the crew of the Niña and the Pinta from a storm which nearly wrecked them on the return journey after the discovery of America.

The Virgin looks today much as she did to the Extremadura adventurers. She is about a metre (yard) in height and all you can see of her is her face for the rest is covered with richly woven garments which conceal the fact that she is, in fact, a seated figure. It is interesting to reflect on the enormous power of this small dark faced symbol on Spain's identity, the Hispanidad, which binds all people of Spanish origin from Spain to the Philippines. In all parts of the

121

Spanish-speaking world there are shrines to the Virgin of Guadalupe; islands, town, cities and mountains are named after her, and once a percentage of all the treasures of America were set aside for her. The first place outside Spain to be named Guadalupe was the West Indian island dedicated by Columbus to his protector.

In Spain the Virgin is kept in the church of Guadelupe high above the altar. Behind her is the treasury – 'Camarin' – in which are kept the jewels and costumes given to her and which are worn on special occasions. The day of Hispanidad October 12 is the most notable occasion and the day when she is carried in a procession around the village.

The keypoint of Guadalupe is its church and the monastic buildings which crowd around it. These include a cloister in Mudéjar style and another in the Gothic manner, a chapter house containing a unique collection of illuminated medieval books and a sacristy with Zurbarán paintings of the priors of the monastery. The village itself is ancient, its balconied houses overhanging narrow streets, and pigs and chickens allowed to run wild in courtyards and even outside, ignored by all except visitors who come from every corner of the Spanish-speaking world.

It is possible that the presence of the miraculous virgin whose image was in the hearts and minds of all the Spanish soldiers, sailors and merchants who travelled in the vast Spanish Empire, had something to do with Charles V's decision to end his days at the nearby monastery of Yuste, near Jarandillo de la Vera. The Emperor Charles V, Charles I of Spain, son of Philip the Handsome and Joan, called 'the Mad', daughter of Ferdinand and Isabella, ruler of the Hapsburg Empire abdicated his power on 25 October 1555 and retired to the monastery of **Yuste** near Jarandilla da la Vera. The event shook the world and one cannot help wondering what made Europe's most powerful ruler who also held sway over most of South America give up his task as well as his mission to unite the whole of Europe into one political entity ruled by him and one spiritual kingdom ruled by the Pope.

His abdication took place five months after the death of his mother whom, many years before he had persuaded to give up her legal claim to the throne of Spain, keeping her virtually a prisoner at Tordesilas for 46 years. Did, one wonders, Charles V ponder such matters as he meditated at Yuste with his court of 100 servants? Did he also think of the devastation and the economic ruin caused by his ambitions; the sack of Rome, the wars aginst France and England, the campaign against the Protestants? It must have been evident to him that the world he had schemed to create was beginning to collapse. Protestantism was gaining ground all over northern Europe, English and French sea power was making the seas unsafe for his treasure galleons from the New World, and his European Empire was in danger both from within and from the Turks who had taken Istanbul and were advancing into Austria.

Today the sick, gouty Emperor and his ambitious dreams seem far away as you look across the fields of tobacco, red peppers and olive trees towards the old castle where Charles stayed while his monastic quarters were being built. The castle is now a parador named after Charles V. It still possesses the drawbridge and walls he knew and his coat-of-arms hangs among those of the nobility of his day in the impressive courtyard.

From Jarandilla de la Vera the road meanders westward to **Plasencia** which stands on the edge of the Extremadura plateau on a rocky hill above the River Jerte. The town and its cathedral look impressive from a distance but are a little disappointing on closer inspection. The 16th-century Gothic Cathedral was never completed and the ramparts, which look promising from afar, have been gradually absorbed into the fabric of the houses. The old quarter of the town is worth a visit for its fine old houses with wrought-iron grilles evoke the time when Plasencia was a frontier town built to encourage the well-to-do to settle in this part of Spain.

The River Tagus crosses Extremadura to the south and its waters are now used for irrigation by a series of dams, the llargest of which is at Alcántara near the Portuguese border.

123

Below the dam, and now spanning a dry gorge, is the bridge that the Emperor Hadrian ordered to be built in 105 and which the Arabs called Al Kantara.

Cáceres the provincial capital of Extremadura, lies to the south of the River Tagus and still retains almost intact its medieval centre. Much of Cáceres wealth came from the Americas, so it is appropriate that one of the old houses open to visitors today is the Casa de Toledo Montezuma, home of Juan Carno, one of Cortes' lieutenants who married a daughter of Montezuma. The house is at the north-east end of the old city near the Plaza General Mola, named after one of Franco's officers. In the square stands the Torre Butaco, a Roman tower used during festivals as a launch pad for fireworks.

Inside the medieval walls are tightly packed streets of 15- and 16th-century houses, many of them belonging to noble families who were members of the Order of Santiago, a military society of knights dedicated to the protection of pilgrims travelling to the shrine of St James at Santiago di Compostela.

Near the Casa de Toledo Montezuma is the Church of Santa Maria set in an elegant square with the same name. On the same side of the square as the church is a fine 15th-century house, the Palacio de los Golfines de Abajo, a palace in which Ferdinand and Isabella stayed more than once. Walking westward from the palace you pass the Church and College of San Francisco to reach the Plaza San Mateo. This was formerly the Arabs' quarter of the city, in which stands the impressive Church of St Matthew (**San Mateo**), a Gothic structure built between the 14th and the 16th century which contains the tombs of some of the noble families who lived in Cáceres.

On the south side of the square is an interesting relic of the time when Spain was full of feuding nobility. This is the Home of the Storks, (**Casa de las Cigueñas**) which has managed to retain the machicolated tower which Isabella ordered all nobles to eliminate from their homes in an attempt to reduce rivalry and to make them put Spain before their private interests.

124

Modern Cáceres extends far beyond the old medieval walls and is a busy city, especially on market days in May and September when the farmers of Extremadura gather for the sale of cattle, sheep and pigs.

Some 47 kms (30 miles) to the east of Cáceres lies **Trujillo,** a very similar city, with its old quarter rising above the main town on a granite hillside on which is perched a formidable castle. Like Cáceres, Trujillo has many fine buildings but, being of later construction, they have a less defensive look and are bright with flower-bedecked balconies and painted facades. The centre of the town is the Plaza Mayor, an unusual arcaded square with irregular sides and tiers of steps. In its centre is a fearsome looking equestrian statue of Francisco Pizarro, conqueror of the Incas, which was made in 1927 by an American sculptor.

Mérida

Some 90 k to the south west of Trujillo lies Mérida where there are substantial remains of the Roman town of Emerita Augusta. Built by Agrippa, son-in-law of Augustus Caesar, the town was the capital of Western Spain. Today this small Extremadura town is a tranquil place on the River Guadiana whose social life centres on the cafés of the Plaza de España. For the visitor this is a blessing for you enjoy the relics of the ruined Roman town without the maddening crowds of the popular tourist towns.

The principal ruins lie in the north east corner of the town and consist of the **Roman Arena** which seated some 14,000 people and the **Theatre.** Under the arena are the quarters reserved for the gladiators and pens for the wild animals used in the performances. A passageway connects the arena to the **Theatre** whose long colonnaded stage still survives. Built by Agrippa the theatre could accommodate an audience of 5,000.

Nearby in Calle J Ramon Mélide is the **Museum of Roman art** where Roman finds from statuary to glassware are on show, and below the arena are the floors of a Roman villa whose mosaics and tiling are well preserved.

The Roman Circus to the north of the town has unfortunately almost entirely disappeared but to the north west there are the considerable remains of a **Roman acqueduct** (Aqueducto de Los Milagros) which once supplied the town which was twice as large as the one that one sees today. In Merida as in other old Roman towns the buildings were the quarries for the stone used or other buildings. Many of those have ended up in the Alcazaba fortress by the **Roman bridge** that crosses the Guadiana River.

☆ ☆ ☆ ☆ ☆

The Conquistadors

Extremadura was the breeding ground of the Conquistadors who took possession of Central and South America and established the vast overseas Spanish Empire. They did so with small bands of soldiers and followers who penetrated into unknown country and found themselves surrounded by thousands of armed Indians. The Conquistadors were tough men from a hard country, many were uneducated and they came from a Europe where warfare was a merciless business. To survive in the alien territory in which they found themselves they adopted ruthless and what seems to us today barbarous methods. However, if you take account of the times which they lived and the particular situation they faced it is hard to see what else they could have done. The Conquistadors were followed by others with more peaceful though equally self interested motives. These were the priests with their mission of making the Indians into good loyal Spanish Catholics and the colonizers and businessmen who, after the first mad rush for gold, wanted to make the Americas a productive commerical extension of Spain.

The first certain proof that a new continent had been discovered was when Vasco Nuñez de Balboa, who was born at Jerez de los Caballeros in south west Extremadura, fought and hacked his way through the tropical jungles of the Isthmus of Panama and saw the Pacific Ocean. This was a feat which John Keats attributed to Cortés.

"Or like stout Cortcz, when with eagle eyes
He stared at the Pacific-and all his men
Look'd at each other with a wild surmise-
Silent upon a peak in Darien."

Soon after, Cortés arrived in Mexico and with a force of only 450 men marched to the Aztec capital at Tenochtitlan, today's Mexico City. Hernan Cortés was an educated man who had attended the university of Salamanca and at first he tried to achieve his conquest by diplomacy. However, he was dealing with a vast Empire split within itself by warring factions. What is more his Spanish religious zeal and perhaps his humanitarian instincts led him to replace the blood sodden idols of the Aztecs with effigies of the Virgin which aroused the enmity of the Indian priesthood. This led the Aztec Montezuma's brothers to stage a revolt in which most of Cortés troops were massacred. With the help of the Mascala Indians who were enemies of the Aztecs Cortés retreated and regrouped his forces. Later he returned to take Tenochtitlan and was made Captain General of New Spain, as Mexico was named. However, as with most of the Conquistadors his enemies were not only among the Indians but also among other envious Spaniards. He was recalled to Spain in 1528 where he was made a Marquis by Charles V but subsequently his governorship was taken from him. In the melée of the rush to the Americas Cortes was soon forgotten and died in poverty near Seville. His body now lies at Tezcuzco, Mexico.

The conquest of South America was a more drawn out and barbarous affair than that of Mexico and largely carried out by Francisco Pizarro with his brothers who came from the vicinity of Trujillo. Francisco was the bastard of the family and spent his early life as a swineherd. Without any education and surrounded by a society within which feudal lords thought nothing of massacring whole villages and burning their houses to the ground Francisco was conditioned to the idea that life was a hard business with little mercy for those who did not know how to survive.

When therefore he arrived in Peru and began his march into the Empire of the Incas in 1532 he was not lulled into a sense of security by the fact that the Indians did not at first appear aggressive. He knew that the Inca chief Atahualpa was a usurper and that his Empire included tribes who were opposed to Atahualpa's reign. In these uncertain conditions Pizarro decided that the best defence was offence and at his meeting with the Inca chief at Cajamarca, he and his 170 men took the Indian forces by surprise and within two hours had slaughtered some six thousand of them and taken Atahualpa prisoner. Pizarro then offered the Inca chief his freedom if he would fill one of the rooms in his palace with gold. A year later this was accomplished but Atahualpa was strangled just the same.

The gold which Pizarro now sent back to Spain aroused gold fever wherever it stopped. Soon the whole of north and west South America began to be filled with treasure seeking Spaniards as well as some Germans of the Welser trading family whose importance can be gauged even today by the Fondaco Tedeschi, the German trading headquarters in Venice near the Rialto bridge, which they built.

The story of the search for Inca gold, told by Dr John Hemming in **The Search for Eldorado**, preoccupied many Spaniards and others for centuries to come. Meanwhile other expeditions ranged around South America trying to discover and conquer more territories. Among these was the Pizarro expedition down the west coast to Chile which was actually led and organised by Diego de Almagro, a foundling from Extremadura. Almagro's journey over the deserts of northern Chile is an epic of endurance and barbarity but it achieved little. Chile was poor country which even the Incas had largely ignored and the pickings were poor. Moreover it was peopled by a warlike tribe of Araucanian Indians who remained unconquered even when Pedro de Valdivia began the colonization of Central Chile, founding the city of Santiago in 1541.

Meanwhile other explorations were taking place, Francisco de Orellana, born in Trujillo, a lieutenant of Pizarro, crossed the Andes in Peru and followed the Amazon down to its mouth. Earlier in 1516 Juan Diaz de Solis had explored the River Plate (**Rio de la Plata**) and Diego de Ordas, a knight of Santiago had tried to find his way to the mythical El Dorado on the River Orinoco. On the way he discovered the raging Atura rapids (which were negotiated by Hovercraft in another daring expedition in 1968).

The daring exploits and the suffering of the early Conquistadors brought few of them either happiness or wealth. Almagro was defeated in a battle with Pizarro on his return from Chile and strangled but later avenged by his halfcaste son who stormed Pizarro's stronghold and killed him. Pedro de Valdivia was killed by Indians at the battle of Tucapel. Only Hernando Francisco Pizarro's brother enjoyed the fruits of the conquest of the west coast of South America. He created , in Trujillo, the building now known as the Palacio de la Reconquista and lived there with this brother's Inca princess wife.

Chapter Six:
The orchards of the south east

Though the Mediterranean coast of Spain south of the Ebro to Valencia was once part of Catalonia and Castilian influence used to be strong in Murcia, the people of the south-east have developed their own independent character. The Levant consists of a separate enclave encircled by the mountains of the central cordillera to the north and those of Andalucía to the south.

Like the Catalans, the people of the Levant were a maritime trading community looking eastwards to the commercial world of the Mediterranean and its links with Asia through the Middle East. Like most maritime people, they had an outward-looking, adventurous and inquisitive spirit, far more so than the inhabitants of the Spanish meseta who were preoccupied with the internal politics of their inland kingdom and their dynastic strategies with the countries of Europe across the Pyrenees.

When Aragon allied itself with Catalonia and subsequently became a partner with Castile the loose political structure of the maritime western seaboard was no match for the Castilian central power. When Castile, in its turn, backed the great American adventure the Levant, like Catalonia, declined in importance.

Nevertheless, the individuality and independence of the maritime peoples of the Levant, as of Catalonia, remained and it is not coincidence that in the subsequent history of Spain these regions were often hotbeds of resistance and revolt against the central government whenever it tried to deprive the maritime states of their rights.

Though the loss of maritime power was a blow to the eastern seaboard, in the Levant, at least, the people had another valuable asset in the rich soil of the lowlands of Valencia. The Moors did a great deal in this region to develop irrigation systems and to set up agriculture. Their expulsion brought stagnation which added to the region's difficulties so that for centuries it was by-passed by the main stream of Spanish life which flowed through the Atlantic ports and the central cities. In the 20th century there has been something of a Renaissance in this part of Spain. The restoration of the irrigation systems, improved techniques in farming and a growing demand throughout Europe for the products of its fruit orchards and market gardens allied to the development of holidays resorts along formerly deserted coasts has brought wealth to the Levant.

Valencia

The chief city of the Levant is Valencia whose chequered career goes back to the time of the early Mediterranean traders who made landfalls on the coast here. Phoenecians, Greeks, Carthaginians, Romans, Visigoths and Arabs all landed and traded here and some of them settled, thus giving the population rich ethnic roots. In 1409 the city, which was in the hands of the Moors, was taken by El Cid who made it his fief until his death. Later, it was retaken by the Moors and finally liberated permanently by Jaime the Conqueror, of Catalonia.

The old city of Valencia, built along the River Turia, was surrounded by a wall: most of which has now disappeared, except for two gates, one, the Torres de Quart on the west side, and the more imposing Torre de Serranos built in 1398 to the north and facing the river. From the Serranos gate you can quickly reach the centre of the old city. You go along the Calle de Serranos which leads to the Calle de Caballeros and the 15th century Provincial Council building (**Generalidad**), which has a magnificently colonnaded patio and spacious halls hung with portraits of the kings and queens of Aragon and of Spain. Behind the Generalidad across the Plaza de

132

Manises is another of Valencia's great mansions, the Palace of the Marquess of Scala.

At the eastern end of the Calle de Caballeros is the Plaza de la Virgen, an attractive though busy square with a Neptune fountain overlooked by the northern end of Valencia's Cathedral. The west front of the **Cathedral** has a particularly fine portal, the Puerta de los Apóstoles, with figures of some of the apostles and an intricate rose window above.

If you are passing this door on a Thursday you may well notice a meeting taking place under it. At first glance the group of people, seems to be a social one, friends of the cathedral, perhaps. The men, some in shirt sleeves, others wearing black peasant smocks, sit behind a wrought-iron enclosure in quiet or animated conversation. A hint that this is more than just an informal meeting is given by the crowds listening to their words, some of them even recording their conversation on transistors. The occasion is, in fact, the weekly meeting of the Tribunal de las Aguas, a body of men elected to act as judges in all disputes regarding the distribution of water, the life blood of the **huertas** (market gardens and orchards) on which the prosperity of the Valencia region depends.

A walk past them and along the Calle Miguelete which flanks the church brings you to the simple main facade of the Cathedral and the free-standing Miguelete Tower ('Micalet' to the Valencians). If you have the energy it is worth while climbing to the top of the tower for a fine view of Valencia and the Mediterranean sea beyond.

The interior of the Cathedral shows a mixture of styles and has little of outstanding interests, though the view of the Cimborrio **dome** which rises over the crossing is architecturally charming. The huge tracery windows allow in more light than usually found in Spanish churches – enough to illuminate the high altar's large painted panels showing scenes from the life of the Virgin painted by Almedian and Llanos who were disciples of the Leonardo da Vinci style. Other paintings in the cathedral include works by Ribera, Fiorentino and Goya.

El Cid's harsh sense of justice is also illustrated by the story of the counts of Carrion de las Cordes who married El Cids daughers for their dowry and then treated them cruelly, and abandoned them. El Cid sought out the avaracious knights who were killed. Their widows later made better marriages to nobles from Aragon and Navara.

To the north of the Cathedral is the Chruch of the Virgin of the Forsaken (**Basilica de la Virgen de los Desamparados**) – the Virgin is the patron saint of Valencia.

The part of Valencia to the east of the Cathedral has many interesting and grand old mansions and churches including the house of St Joseph Ferrer who became famous for his fiery sermons which helped convert large number of Moors and Jews to Christianity.

In the western quarter of the city is the Market Square (**Plaza del Mercado**) and the old silk market, (**La Lonja.**) This is one of the finest buildings in Valencia and evidence of the the importance of the silk trade which Valencian merchants developed in the 17th century as a result of their contacts with eastern Mediterranean trade. The Lonja complex is in two sections, in the centre of which is the tower with its delicate tracery and gothic windows, and with columns decorated with animals and human figures.

Across the street you can enjoy a visit to the modern market. It is housed in a domed building gleaming with tiles, where crowds of shoppers test the quality of the produce or argue with the stall holders: a wonderful morning's entertainment for those who enjoy watching other people's daily lives.

The huge church that dominates the Plaza is the Church of the Saints John (**Iglesia de los Santos Juanes**) which is in a rather dilapidated state, partly because of the wear and tear of time and partly because of damage caused during the Civil War. Like so many churches everywhere in Europe, this one was not improved during the baroque period by the addition of tons of clumsy stucco work.

The modern social and workaday life of Valencia goes on in the southern part of the old city around the vast Plaza del Pais Valenciano, a well-kept, roughly triangular open space well planted with trees and flowers. Cafés, restaurants and shops abound in the surrounding streets which have the usual traffic problems of all modern cities. The Square is dominated by two large buildings, the Municipal Council and historical museum of Valencia in the south-west corner and, opposite, the Post Office (**Correos y Telégrafos**), a public service which always seems to be sumptuously housed in Spain.

More of the city's grand or grandiose – according to your taste – buildings lie to the north of the plaza. Among them, by the church of the Sacred Cross Santa Cruz, is the House of the Marquess of the Two Rivers (**Palacio de Marques de Dos Aguas**), and 18th-century palace in high baroque style with an agitated portal portraying the Virgin bathed in carved rays of light among writhing angels. The building now houses the national collection of ceramics.

Nearby is the College of the Patriarch, (**Colegio de Patriarca**), who was Juan de Ribera, Archbishop of Valencia who also became the Patriarch of Antioch. He had more classical than baroque tastes and the building is in Renaissance style with some fine courtyards. It also incorporates the Church of Corpus Christi which is in the restrained manner of the Temple of the Escorial.

Though many of the churches of Valencia may be too exuberantly designed for many people's taste, the art collection across the river in the provincial Art Museum (**Museo Provincial de Bellas Artes** on the San Pio V riverside boulevard must be enjoyed by everyone, for here is one of the finest collections in Spain with pictures ranging from the primitive to those of the Golden Age of Spanish painting. There is also a collection of archaeological finds from the region.

☆ ☆ ☆ ☆ ☆

El Cid of Valencia

El Cid Campeador, whose real name was Rodrigo de Vilar is a Spanish folk hero of magnificent stature but for outsiders he seems no more than a medieval adventurer looking for opportunities for his own advantage and as ready to ally himself with the Christians as with the Moors. A traveller in Spain cannot ignore this larger than life hero for his legend and his aura are interwoven into the fabric of the national soul. One comes across El Cid in stories of his exploits throughout Spain and there are traces of his existence from Cantabria to the Levant. Who then was this man who had the qualities of audacity, courage, chivalry, gentleness, loyalty which Spanish people admire and could also be as ruthless as any of his enemies.

He was born in 1043 in Vivar a small village near Burgos and in his early years seems to have been a loyal soldier of Sancho the Great of Castile, who when Sancho was murdered by Alfonso switched his allegiance to the new sovereign who arranged for him to marry Jimena Diaz daughter of the Count of Oviedo.

Domestic life did not however suit the great adventurer so he offered his services to Count Berenguer of Barcelona and having been turned down then joined Moctadir, the Moorish king of Zaragoza. This evidence of his mercenary and, in modern terms, treasonable activities should however be interpreted in the context of his times when Spain was not nation but a land ruled by feudal lords some Christian and some Moorish.

During the succeeding years El Cid continued to serve the Moors sometimes against other Moorish lords and sometimes against Christians. His reputation as a general meanwhile increased and he began to be known throughout Spain as El Campeador, a champion in the art of war which was an indispensable attainment of any medieval squire who wanted to get on in life.

Like most mercenary knights El Cid no doubt had his mind set on winning a kingdom for himself as well as serving Spanish and Moorish kings. His opportuntiy came when the Almoravid Moors began to advance up the peninsula. Valencia was then ruled by Cadir a weak vassal of King Alfonso VI of Castile who was unlikely to be able to withstand the Almoravid onslaught. With great guile El Cid set out for Valencia on the pretext of protecting Cadir while King Alfonso was busy resisting the new Moorish advance in south west Spain. The battle for Valencia was fierce and drawn out and, according to some sources, El Cid was ruthless with his enemies feeding prisoners to dogs or burning them alive. Finally having surrounded the city he imposed a siege which gradually deprived the population of food. Those who became refugees were turned back into the city to starve; eventually the city gave in and the Moorish Cadi of Valencia was burned at the stake.

Once in Valencia El Cid became its ruler and brought his wife and his children from Vivar to share his new kingdom. His reign was shortlived for he died in 1099. El Cid's widow tried to stay on in the Alcázar but she was unable to resist the renewed Moorish attacks and finally left, with El Cid's remains, and returned to Castile.

His exploits lived on however and the super hero image of El Cid no doubt fired the imagination of the Christian armies which eventually drove the Moors not only out of the Valencia but the whole of Spain.

☆ ☆ ☆ ☆ ☆

Inland Levant

The green land of the low-lying coastal **huertas** of the Levant is blessed with almost all-the-year-round sunshine and with a copious supply of river water from the high sierras which make the alluvial soil the most productive in Spain. Where the mountains rise to the meseta in the west the greenery soon fades away and stony hillsides take over. These dry, rugged hills have always been both a frontier between the coast and the inland plateau of Castile, a depopulated area where the rocky earth does not support much life and where the sparse villages have always played a defensive role in the struggles that have taken place over the Levant.

In the north sierras which separate Catalonia from the Levant the town of **Morella,** with its castle and mile-long ramparts, was built as an early strongpoint in the gradual march southwards of the Christians against the Moors. At 1004 metres (3294 ft) it is in a commanding position and has defended itself against Moors and the Barbary pirates that raided the coast. The control of this and other fortresses along this region was given to the Knights of Montesa by James II of Aragon and from here they made incursions south, acquiring Moorish lands as they went.

Present-day Morella is a quiet place which has retained much of its medieval character. The main way into the town through St Michael's Gateway, (**Puerta San Miguel**) leads into steep, narrow streets bordered by ancient houses which appear almost deserted. Down in the valley the old aqueduct, of which there are substantial remains, sits solitary in the sunshine, no longer used except by a goat or two that huddle in its shade.

The solitude of Morella extends all the way down the mountainous interior of the Levant as far as the **huertas** of Valencia where the green orchards and market gardens, the orange trees and almonds provide a refreshing contrast to the dry hills.

Beyond the fertile plain where Turia and Júcar rivers flow there are more hills and fortified towns close to the **huertas.** Two of these, **Gandia** and **Játiva,** are associated with one of the most notorious of papal families. The Borjas (Borgias) – as they were called in Spain – won their land by service to Ferdinand and never looked back. In the days when politics and the Church were almost synonymous the Borjas, with their skills at diplomacy and their pragmatic minds, soon became pillars of the religious establishment, producing no fewer than two Popes, seven cardinals, eight bishops and even one saint.

Alexander VI, father of Lucretia who married into the Este family of Ferrara, and of Cesare whose audacious and ruthless exploits consolidated the Papal dominions from the Tyrrenhian to the Adriatic, was born in Játiva, the more interesting of the two Borgia towns. The castle at Játiva, built on Roman and Moorish foundations, was known to the Borgias, though they spent little time in the town of their birth. Pope Calixtus, the only Borgia to return to his native land, is buried in Játiva's 16th-century Renaissance church. His palace, known as the 'palace of the Saintly duke' (**Palacio del Santo Duque**), is at Gandia.

By the time that Francis Borgia entered the Church, its worst perils after the impoverishment that followed the Schism and which threatened the Papacy of Alexander VI were over. By then Francis was thirty-six and had fathered eight children. His wife's death led him to give up the material life. He handed all his property to his son and devoted himself to building up the then little known order of the Jesuits. His success in this new life brought him to the head of the order as Father General and when he died it was said that he was as much mourned by ordinary people as by the high-ranking members of the Church.

His palace is now a Jesuit College but is open to visitors; it has a fine Gothic patio and some elegantly decorated rooms with painted and cloisonné ceilings and marble-tiled floors.

South of Játiva, some 50 km (30 miles) away along a winding road, is the town of **Alcoy,** on the river of the same name and surrounded by the Sierra Montcabrer. Though now a small industrial town, Alcoy has kept a certain regional charm and much of its traditional architecture. In fact, Alcoy is strong on tradition and proud of the part it played in the stormy years of the Reconquest. Every April it celebrates the battles of the Moors and Christians in a festival called Moros y Christianos (see page 00).

Inland some 36 k (22 miles) from Alcoy is **Villena** in the centre of a fertile **huerta.** Named after the adviser and ally of Henry IV and his illegitimate daughter La Beltraneja, Villena still possesses a castle whose walls and keep are intact. The town has some fine stone mansions with noble coats of arms that evoke its past but today it is a quiet place.

The former strategic importance of this area of the Levant is evident from its large number of castles and fortified villages, among them Biar to the east and Sax and La Mola on the road to Elche to the south.

Elche is a most unusual place and a traveller might well think that he had been transported suddenly to north Africa on finding himself in the forest of palm trees that lie near Elche. Planted originally by either Visigoths or Moors, the palm plantations do a brisk business selling palm fronds all over Spain for Palm Sunday. The leaves are plaited into various traditional shapes, often that of a cross, and kept throughout the year; sometimes, whole fronds are pinned to the fronts of houses or on to balconies to protect the inhabitants during the year.

There have been many different races at Elche and archaeological digs have turned up some interesting finds, the most famous of which is the Lady of Elche, (**Dama de Elche**) a bust of probably Ibero-Greek origins, now in the Madrid Archaeological Museum. Most of the excavations are at **La Alcudia,** an interesting site where finds are exhibited at the local museum.

In the deep south of the Levant where it borders on Andalucía the land becomes a semi-desert again, except for the area round the town of **Murcia** which is situated among the **huertas** of the Segura river valley. In the 13th century the Bishop of Cartagena moved his headquarters to Murcia as he regarded the recaptured town safe from pirate attacks. Murcia flourished as a political centre and a commercial base for the silk trade for which it cultivated silkworms fed on the leaves of its mulberry trees.

Though it suffered during the Napoleonic Wars and more recently during the Civil War, Murcia has some noteworthy buildings, including the Cathedral of Santa María, a 15th-century building rebuilt in the 18th after flood damage. Baroque in style, it has a fine facade and tower and enough stone swags, pediments and saints making dramatic gestures to amuse the eye agreeably as you sit in the plaza in front of it.

There are a number of churches in Murcia, most of them dating from the 17th and 18th centuries, though some are older and were refurbished during that florid period. There is also a considerable collection of paintings and polychrome statuary at the Hermitage of Jesus (**Ermita de Jesus**) which is worth looking at if you have time to spare.

The Costa del Azahar and Costa Blanca

The two costas of the Levant have much beautiful scenery, some of which has been spoilt by the overdevelopment of tourist resorts. Mountains and plains alternate, providing a rich landscape of cliffs, promontories and **huertas** which stretch from the edge of the shore inland to the mountains. The ports and harbours scattered along the coast all have a long history for this was the shore where Phoenicians, Greeks and Romans arrived to trade and where fuedal lords built fortresses and castles to protect their lands from invaders and pirates as well as from the Moors.

One of the most striking of these fortress ports is **Peñiscola** in the far north of the Levant. The fortress is built on a craggy promontory and the town huddles around it for protection behind the seawalls that encircle the peninsula. An unforgettable sight on those cloudless days which the Levant is blessed with for most of the year.

The port was captured from the Moors in 1233 by Jaime I of Aragon who gave it to Knights Templars and they built the castle there in the 14th century. When this powerful military order was abolished, the castle passed to the crown of Castile. During the following century the fortress was the home of the Antipope Benedict XIII who, despite the end of the Schism and the reinstatement of a pope in Rome, refused to give up his papal appointment made by French Bishops and recognized in Spain. During the War of the Spanish Succession Peñiscola remained loyal to the Bourbon Philip V and was rewarded with municipal rights. Its last taste of action was in 1814 when it was taken by the French, who resisted Spanish attempts to recapture it. The castle has been restored and is worth a visit, not only for its handsome rooms but also for the superb views from its buildings.

To the south of Peñiscola is the most northerly of the Levant tourist developments at Benicásim; then you reach **Castellón de la Plana,** a town which stands slightly inland amidst a fertile **huerta.** Much damaged during the Civil War, Castellón has a relatively modern appearance, though its old church with its separate town still stands, as does the Town Hall, which has an attractive 17th-century facade.

The port of Castellón is called El Grau, a generic name for all landing places in the western Mediterranean. This is a lively little place with plenty of picturesque activity as the ships load fruit, oranges and vegetables from the **huertas.**

Other products of the region shipped from here are tiles (**azulejos**) and **alpargatas,** those Spanish rope-soled sandals which are so comfortable to wear in hot weather.

Travelling on south towards Valencia, one passes the road that leads to the grottoes of Saint Joseph (**Grutas de San José**). These grottoes, near **Vall de Uxo,** can be explored by boat along a subterranean river cave some 1200 yards long and have weirdly shaped stalactites and eroded rocks.

Further south along the coast road is historic **Sagunto,** now a small town on the River Palencia which still has its castle perched on a dramatic crag behind the white houses of the town. The ruins are extensive and include remnants of the wall built by the first Iberian settlers. There are also Roman remains, including a theatre, built during Punic Wars. As the battle raged, the inhabitants of Sagunto rather than surrender to Hannibal instead built a pyre on which all women and children committed suicide, while the men sallied forth to their deaths at the hand of the Carthaginians.

Later, during the wars against the Moors, the citadel was taken by El Cid, but it did not finally become part of Christian Spain until 1238. The town's last historical role was as the place from which Alfonso XII was proclaimed King in 1874 after the Republican revolt of 1873 had failed.

Beyond Sagunto lies the great fertile plain of Valencia. To the south of which lies the vast sweetwater lake of La Albufera, separated from the sea by a sand bar and surrounded by rice fields which supply the rice not only for the Valencian dish of **Paella a la Valenciana,** a succulent concoction of rice, chicken and shellfish, but for a good export trade too. The lake is also a pleasure park with boats for hire and sportsmen gather here to shoot the gamebirds.

The Costa del Azahar comes to an end at the promontory called Cabo de San Antonio, a rocky area with attractive resorts being developed at Denia and Jávea amid tree-covered hills. Across a bay is Cabo de Nao, the eastern end of the Andalucian mountain range which disappears under the sea here to emerge as the island of Ibiza.

Beyond the promontories the coast turns south-west and becomes the **Costa Blanca.** The road climbs over the promontory through a lovely spur of mountains whose high point is Guadalest, an area of rocky pinnacles and pines and palm from which there are many exhilarating views over the sea.

The road now winds down steeply to what was once a small fishing village but is now the star resort of south-east Spain: **Benidorm.** Like other internationally famous resorts of the Spanish costas, Benidorm arouses as many partisan emotions as the bullfight. It is large, its high-rise buildings imitate such other centres of contemporary hedonism as Miami and Torremolinos, it has two sandy beaches and endless bars as well as a wealth of places of entertainment. It satisfies all those who enjoy themselves best when surrounded by thousands of others like themselves and no doubt it will continue to be a success as long as the fashion for sea, sun and propinquity continues.

The Benidorm effect has also spread along other parts of the nearby coastline to **Altea,** where there is a charming old village around church on a hillside behind the modern resort along the shore. Also to **Calpe,** where the hotels spread along the coast near a huge craggy rock called the **Peñon de Ifach** 1089 ft (332 m) high which can be climbed and is popularly compared to the Rock of Gibraltar.

The main town of the Costa Blanca is **Alicante,** an important port situated between two large spurs of hills which has a busy businesslike air about it. Down at the port the cranes load crates of fruit, wine and some of the products of the industrial development in metallurgical and chemical products. Along the Esplanada de España's mosaic pavements businessmen as well as tourists mingle. The high rise buildings are offices and apartments as well as hotels. The city's cathedral of San Nicholas, with splendid gilded altars with gilt grilles, is attended by worshippers rather than visitors. Alicante is in fact a city with its own life and has flourished since the Romans and Carthaginians had a base on the strategic high ground occupied by the Castle of Santa Barbara.

There is also a holiday aspect to Alicante by the shore on its northern edge where large hotels and a fine beach, Playa

143

del Postiguet under the castle crag, provide all the amenities of a seaside resort.

South of Alicante there are also coastal resorts being developed. These reach a climax at the **Manga del Mar Menor** a vast sea lagoon surrounded by mushrooming holiday villages. Here the coast which curves around the peninsula of Cabo de Palos to the west has acquired the name of **Costa Calida** – the warm coast – which hardly differentiates it from all the other Spanish costas. However, the coastal area of Murcia does have a character of its own. The terrain is mountainous to the very edge of the sea except for the area round La Manga. It has cliffs and headlands, sheltered coves and rocky ravines in which palms and oleanders grow and the cicadas keep up their evocative music among the dry grasses.

The only port along this rugged coast is **Cartagena** which received its name from the Carthaginians. Surrounded by the steep Sierra del Algarrobo the harbour has sheltered shipping vessels since before it was fought over by Romans and Carthaginians. In medieval times it was too exposed to private attacks and when the bishopric was removed to Murcia it lost its former importance. Later it regained some of its former glory when Philip II built the fortress which stood where the public gardens above the harbour are today. More recently it has recouped some of its importance as a trading port as a result of the development of an oil refinery at nearby Escombreras.

Chapter Seven:
Island beach resorts

Fifty years ago the Balearic Islands were a quiet, little known group of islands where the inhabitants made a living from agriculture, fishing and ceramics. A few visitors arrived from Barcelona by steamer and stayed at old hotels in Palma, Mahon or Ibiza town. Most of them spent a good deal of their time exploring the interior of the island, studying the flora and fauna, the ancient buildings and some of them bathed on the sandy beaches.

Since then the Balearics have become the most popular holiday islands in the world. Some three million visitors arrive every year, mostly by air, and they are catered for in large urban developments with gigantic concrete hotels, each one of which holds more inhabitants than most of the towns and villages on the islands. The total number of visitors far exceeds the population of Balearic peoples which numbers less than a million.

The tourist invasion has had a greater effect on the Balearic people than did some two centuries of occupation by the Moors. In 1229 James 1 of Aragon fought the decisive battle in Palma Bay, in which some 50,000 men died, and restored Christian control of the islands.

The Aragonese through their association with the seagoing Catalans made the islands an important part of the Mediterranean trade system, which included the Aragon colonies in Sicily, the Greek Islands and Crete. When America was discovered the commercial importance of the Balearic Islands began to decline, though the islands continued to be strategic watching posts against the Turks who were threatening the western powers of the Mediterranean. After

the 17th century the islands reverted to quiet places with a
small population of farmers and fishermen who carried on
the struggle for a livelihood that had always been their lot.
Now and again the new maritime powers of England, France
and Holland used them as a base but this hardly affected the
life of the islanders. During the period Minorca became an
English naval headquarters and Nelson himself lived at
Mahon where he spent some of his free time writing a book
Sketches of my Life in 1799.

With the opening of Spain to tourism in the dying years of
the Franco regime the Balearics entered an entirely new era.
Land once almost worthless, became much sought after by
builders of hotels and villas. Farmers turned to market
gardening to satisfy the growing demand for fruit and
vegetables from the visitors, fishermen no longer fished to
satisfy the small demands of local inhabitants but to supply
hotels and restaurants catering for tourists. Labourers and
the casually employed found new jobs in the tourist industry
and the immigrants from Southern Spain who crowded into
Catalonia in search of work found it across the sea in the new
El Dorado. With economic success came problems undreamt
of before which included ugly urban developments in beauty
spots, pollution of the seas and a decline in the once plentiful
shoals of fish and crustacea.

The Island of Majorca (Mallorca)

The Majorca of the holiday makers stretches to the east and
west of Palma in a wall of white, concrete buildings
bordering sandy beaches or perched along dark, rugged
rocks against which the sea surges gently with a tracery of
white surf. From the sea the effect of the gleaming buildings
against the dry, austere landscape is quite dramatic suggest-
ing some Utopian modern kingdom where a life of peace and
leisure waits to greet the tired traveller. A closer look dispels
the illusion of indolence; the roads running along the resorts
are busy with motor cars, coaches, cycles as well as the
occasional horse and cart while the pavements are crowded
with slow going pedestrians in shorts, T-shirts, bathing
costumes, cotton frocks and carrying beach bags, plastic

carriers, plaited mats, straw hats, buckets, newspapers and all the other paraphernalia of the beach. Their route is lined with bars and shops selling all the items they might have forgotten or have never thought of. Also for sale are such desirable souvenirs as shell jewellery, wrought iron table decorations, tiles depicting scenes from a bullfight, castanets, painted tambourines and brilliantly coloured postcards on which the purchasers will tell their friends at home about the joys of being here. Not everyone is active however; at the hotel swimming pools and on the beaches the bodies slump in sensual lethargy induced by the sun and the cumulative effects of icecreams, aperitifs, tapas and the abundant buffets with which hotels regale their guests. This is the life that the millions who visit Majorca come for, like the millions who once travelled to the shrine of Santiago de Compostela they arrive from every part of Europe, though without the rigours of a pilgrimage, and their arrival rejoices the heart of those who cater for them from the delegates of the provincial government to the lowliest beach attendant and even the pickpockets who arrive from all over the world for the summer pickings.

Palma de Majorca

The city of Palma de Majorca is both a modern holiday metropolis and a fine and dignified old town. In the curve of its bay yachts and cruisers of every nation come and go under the eyes of the splendid cathedral which dominates the skyline, and at the Estaciones Maritimas the ferries from Barcelona and the cruise ships from the ports of Europe pause for long enough to allow their passengers a short shore leave.

The old town lies between the two wide avenues of Paseo de Mallorca to the west and Avenida Gabriel along Villa-longa to the east. Along its seafront by the Paseo Uruguay the old town is still protected by its city wall behind which lies **the cathedral** and the ancient Moorish fortress of **La Almudaina.**

The cathedral, begun in 1230, was not completed until the 16th/17th century and is in the Gothic style. Of the original

147

only the Renaissance doorway and the south doorway, El Mirador, remain for the building was damaged by earthquake in 1850 and was rebuilt, though the Gothic style was preserved.

The interior of the cathedral is unusual for Spanish churches for it has an open design without the enclosed choir that often blocks the view of the altar. The columns of the nave soar upwards to the roof without the interruption of a triforum. Admirers of Gaudi's work enjoy the wrought iron baldachino over the high altar which is one of the 18 altars which are worth looking at in the side chapels.

In front of the cathedral facing the tree lined **El Born,** the main avenue of Palma life, once the course of the River Rieira, whose course was moved further west, is the Almudaina. This Moorish fortress was the seat of the Arab kings until the 13th century when it became the palace of the Christian kings; today a large part of it is used by the government of Mallorca though it can be visited on a guided tour.

Across Avenida Antonio Maura, to the west, lies **La Lonja,** the great commercial exhange where much Mallorcan business was transacted when it was built in the 15th century. With its four towers and battlements La Lonja looks like a fortress and no doubt the architect G. Sagrerta (who also sculpted St Peter and St Paul in the cathedral) may have had the constant menance of Turkish fleets in mind. La Lonja is not always open but as there are frequent exhibitions held there access is usually possible.

El Born is a short but elegant avenue with a central mall shaded with splendid palm trees, and one can pass hours sitting at cafés there watching Mallorcan life go by but it is also a good springboard for strolls around the old town. In El Born itself is one of the finest residences in the city. The **Casa de los Marques de Sollerich** was the home of this family in the 18th century and is a perfect example of the life of the nobility who ran Mallorca. Its outstanding features are the loggia and its patio with a double flight of stairs.

Eastward of El Born lies the main area of the old city with its narrow streets and little shops including patisseries which produce ensaimadas, light as air, flaky pastries covered with finely powdered sugar, which are the delight of Mallorcans on special occasions.

The old social centre was the **Plaza Mayor,** whose arcaded houses are typical of plazas throughout the length and breadth of Spain.

To the south of the plaza lie a maze of fascinating streets and two of the major churches of Palma, **Santa Eulalia** and **San Francisco.** Both are Gothic in style though the latter has a remodelled Plateresque front and a carved portal tympanum by Herrera, architect of the Escorial. The church has the tomb of Ramon Lull, a famous Mallorcan scholar priest and missionary who like many of the great medieval religious leaders was a reformed libertine. Lull was martyred, by stoning on an expedition to Africa in 1315.

There are many fine houses in this quarter including the **Casa Oleza** (17th century) the **Casa del Marques del Palmar** (16th century) and there are what remains of the Moorish baths by the old Jewish ghetto of **La Portella.**

The modern quarter of Palma follows the bay westwards to the heights of **El Terreno** a pleasure ground area with restaurants, bars, discos and other places of entertainment where sometimes the tension between overworked waiters and over excited visitors can lead to less harmonious relationships than one would wish. Nevertheless here, especially round **Plaza Gomilla** is all the fun of the fair with shows ranging from flamenco to strip tease.

Also here, a mute reminder of another time is the **Bellver Castle (Castillo Belver)** which Mallorcan Kings built in the 14th century but which later became a prison. Now the castle is a museum with archaelogical finds from all over Mallorca and a superb view of Palma Bay from the terrace.

A popular attraction at Palma for visitors who would like taste of mainland Spain is the **Spanish village (Pueblo Español)** in Calle Andrea Doria between Terreno and the old town. Here there are full scale reproductions of many of Spain's most famous historic buildings including parts of the Alhambra in Granada and El Greco's house in Toledo.

Though many visitors stay in Palma few of the wiser ones

149

will frequent its beaches which, at Terreno, are more overcrowded than fly paper in a butcher's shop in Extremadura. Many of the hotels have swimming pools but for anyone determined to try sea bathing there are the sandy beaches east of Palma like El Arenal and C'an Pastilla or the crowded sandy coves between rocky headlands westwards. At El Terreno beach one would be lucky to find a space to spread out a towel and **Magaluf,** similarly crowded, is the most ambitious of popular resorts with huge hotels that possess every kind of holiday attraction from swimming pools to sauna baths. In the town there are wild west bars, flamenco taverns, English tearooms, Chinese takeaways, American hamburger parlours, discos, night clubs and other forms of holiday comfort mingling in exotic profusion.

Beyond Magaluf the pace slows down a little as the coast becomes more indented and filled with resorts that were once regarded as places to get away from it all.

At **Santa Ponsa,** renowned as the place at which King James I of Aragon landed to liberate Mallorca from the Moors, there is still space on the splendid sandy beach from which to watch bathers and the more adventurous wind surfers and parachute riders over the sea.

Paguera and **Camp de Mar** lie in their own secluded bays and are also busy places in summer. **Puerto de Andraitx** as its name suggests is primarily a port once exclusively for fishing boats but now these are in the minority as fleets of yachts and cruisers have taken advantage of the sheltered waters. The presence of so many amateur sailors in the port gives it a different atmosphere to the resorts near Palma.

The north west coast

From Andraitx to Puerto Soller there is a magnificent drive, a large part of it along a corniche road with great views of the north east coast of Mallorca. On the way to it one passes **Andraitx** village nestling discretely one might say almost invisibly, among the mountains, a good starting point for walks and giving a glimpse of a Mallorca untouched by tourism.

The first breathtaking view of sea and rugged coast comes at **Mirador Ricardo Roca** where there is space to park the car and enjoy the view at leisure.

Skirting the edge of Mt. Galatzo one comes to **Banyalbufar** where the cultivation of tomatoes and vines is carried out on terraces on the mountain side.

Beyond Banyalbufar is a road that climbs over the mountains to **Valldemosa,** a place that quickens the heart for anyone familiar with Chopin's Raindrop prelude. During Chopin's four months stay with the feminist George Sand he wrote of blue skies, but one assumes he also had to put up with some of the rain that inspired the prelude. George Sand, christened Armandien Aurore Lucie Dupin Duderant was a Baroness, and a literary lion huntress who left her husband and two children for the Bohemian society of Paris. She took up with Alfred de Musset who pined with love for her in Venice (at the Danieli hotel) before her affair with Chopin from who she later parted to pursue philosophers and politicians. George Sand who later became a noted novelist wrote **A Winter in Mallorca** during her visit with Chopin. The Monastery of Valldemosa where they stayed has become a place of pilgrimage for visitors and is well worth the journey even for those without an addiction to Chopin preludes or French novels, and there is the voyeuristic pleasure of examining the quarters which Frederic and George occupied in the monastery, which at the time was empty of religious persons.

For those without a car there are regular coaches from Palma; those who are driving can return to the coast road and continue to a more recent literary shrine at **Deya,** home of the late Robert Graves, author among other notable works of the novels about Emperor Claudius.

Graves settled in Mallorca in 1929 and lived there until his death in 198? expect for the Civil War period and during World War II and had a local reputation not only as an author but as a player of main stream jazz. Graves also had a hand in the preservation of the old village of Deya which is on a hill off the main road amid groves of almond and olive

151

trees and no doubt sometimes popped into the simple but rather upmarket hotel Deya at road level.

There is a small beach below the cliffs at Deya and another at Lluch Alcari where there is a small hotel.

Most people end up at **Puerto Soller,** an almost landlocked bay with a mountain background. The tranquil water is ideal for all kinds of amateur boating though people who know all about sailing also end up here. Once thought a bit out of the way Puerto Soller is now fairly crowded in summer though it tends to attract the more sophisticated package holidaymaker.

One of the joys of not having a car at Puerto Soller is that you can arrive by train from Palma, over the limestone mountains and travelling on the local train, a wonderful cartoon strip affair which joins the Puerto to Soller village.

Enjoying the same isolation which Puerto Soller once had is **Sa Calobra** to the north. There is no railway to it and the road winds and plunges in a way that will spoil a holiday for people with a nervous disposition and there is hardly any accommodation worth speaking of, so it really is for those who are detemined to get away from it all, except that day trippers from Puerto Soller arrive by boat.

The coast from Sa Calobra to San Vicente is uninhabited and even the road runs inland and across the north west tip of Mallorca to Puerto Pollensa. A branch road goes off to San Vicente where is a large but well run popular hotel with swimming pools and a beach, and not much else. **Puerto Pollensa** also has good hotels and an excellent beach but is much more of a resort, though not over urbanised. From here a finger of land stretches north east to **Formentor** and its splendid luxury hotel in acres of its own land and surrounded by spectacular cliffs. One can drive to the very tip of Cabo Formentor for the view when one is not enjoying the many amenities and pleasures of Puerto Pollensa, or one can go south round the bay to **Alcudia** port from where steamers leave for Menorca and Barcelona. There are the remains of a Roman theatre at Alcudia and modern entertainment is provided at discos and bars.

The south east coast

The land around Alcudia bay is flat and becomes marshy
south of the port for this is where the mountain ranges of the
north west are left behind and the low level east coast, which
is easily accessible from Palma, begins.

Among the attractions of the east coast are the Caves and
further south the Calas (rock bound estuaries) which provide
secluded, though not deserted, bathing beaches.

At the northern end of this stretch of coast is **Cala Ratjada**
which has a sandy beach and rocky strands which provide
perfect environments for the huge varieties of fish and
shellfish which are the joy of divers whether they use
snorkels or proper diving gear. Most of the Calas are situated
on branch roads of the main road that runs inland which is
also an advantage as far as the arrival of casual visitors is
concerned but there is a considerable, though discreet,
development of the Calas for package holidays so none of
them is as empty as they once were. Off season, however,
one can be relatively alone though restaurants situated on
the edge of a clear blue estuary with hardly any other
buldings in sight tend to put on the canned music as soon as
they get a customer; they do not object however if one tells
them to switch it off.

Why canned music should be considered an essential to
any kind of social intercourse is a mystery. Even live music
can be de trop in certain circumstances, but evidently the
cave business operators do not think so for in both groups of
caves along the east coast, the **Cuevas de Hams** and the
Cuevas de Drach, musicians float about playing Chopin (who
else on Mallorca?). The Cuevas de Drach have the whole
geological spectacle amazingly lit and the musicians on boats
and the whole effect is bizzare, though it does make, as they
say, an unforgettable memory and is worth the money.

Both these calas are near **Porto Cristo** halfway along the
coast and in the same area is a Safari park and an aquarium
for added entertainment. As one travels south more orchards
appear and in Springtime the almond blossoms make a

wonderful spectacle. There is also a certain amount of new industry inland around Felanitx which is one of the centres of the Mallorcan pearl and wine business.

Between Felanitx and Cala d'Or on the coast is the **monastery of San Salvador** which dates back to the 13th century and, like another **monastery at Lluc,** on the north west coast, is in the cell renting business, though the ones you are offered have the more austere aspects ameliorated.

The southern calas of the east coast and the most well known in holiday brochures are Cala d'Or and Cala Ferrera and they get rather crowded in summer.

Despite the summer millions Mallorca is still a place to put on one's holiday list though it is better in the off-season than in the summer holiday period.

Menorca

If you prefer a quiet sandy beach without the buzz of speed boats and the spectacle of a broiling cast of thousands then Menorca is probably more suitable. Here you are more likely to pass the evenings in a bar listening to a guitar player rather than watching a show or jigging to an international pop group; and window shopping will not fill many evenings. It can be windy though but the spurs of cliff help to protect the beaches and shore side outdoor cafés.

Like Mallorca, its sister island, Menorca has two geographical aspects: the north coast is mountainous (Mt Toro 358 m – 1174 ft) and rugged with deep coves with small sandy beaches and the south is flatter with even lines of cliffs and long sandy becaches.

Historically Menorca has led a quiet life since the first Bronze age settlers arrived from the eastern Mediterranean until the English arrived in 1713, having gained possession of it by the Treaty of Utrecht which ended the War of the Spanish Succession. The English changed one or two things such as moving the capital from Cindadela on the west coast to Mahon on the east and introducing the drink called gin, which they found could be made locally with the island's juniper berries, but mostly left the islanders alone.

The Menorcans carried on as they always had farming the small plots of land, building stone walls, and whitewashing the walls of their small cottages and have done so ever since, at least until tourism proved to be a more profitable occupation than farming or fishing.

Mahon

The capital of Menorca is also the port of arrival by ship and air (the airport is 5 km away). Apart from its fame as the headquarters of the English fleet from 1708 to 1783 and as the place of origin of mayonnaise (Mahonaise) during the brief occupation Mahon has little of interest though it has some of the charm of a little English port with its bowfronted houses and steep streets. Down by the harbour is the Plaza de España where, in the early morning there is a lively scene as stalls sell the products of the fishermen's night's work and there is another permanent general market in the Plaza Carmen, in the cloisters of an old Carmelite church. The main church in Mahon is in the Plaza de la Conquista and the Town Hall is in the Town Hall (**Ayuntamiento**) a 17th century building.

Around Menorca

Getting around Menorca's 669 km^2 (258 sq. miles) is not easy unless you have a car and without one it is difficult to reach some of the solitary beaches that are among the pleasures of being in Menorca. Even with a car the beautiful but isolated coves are difficult to find for they are reached by tracks across open fields. A good map is therefore essential.

Having acquired some form of self drive transportation (some people hire mopeds) one can have a wonderful time enjoying splendid picnics a la Robinson Crusoe on secluded beaches or visiting some of the points of local interest.

To the south of Mahon is **Villa Carlos,** an extension of Mahon created by the English under the name of George-town. Admiral Collingwood's house here is now a small hotel and the plaza is the old army parade ground a relic of which are the barrack buildings around it.

From Mahon a number of roads radiate to little resorts along the north and south coast. One of these, on the road to **San Luis,** passes by some of Menorca's megalithic monuments. These were built in the second millenium BC when settlers began to populate Menorcas caves and build houses and primitive temples. The stony remains consist of talayots, large cairns of stone on which, it is belived, wooden structures were erected and taulas, large flat stones resting on other stones like an altar, as in Stonehenge.

Another road goes to **Cala'n Porter** one of the many little settlements around the coast created by the houses to which people from all over Europe have retired or which have been built for letting to summer visitors.

Cala'n Porter is typical of this kind of development: small villas are scattered along the cliffs above a sandy beach. There are a few shops to provide essential needs and more are open in summer with tourist supplies.

A few and restaurants and a cave (**Cova d'en Xoroi**) across the bay which a local entrepreneur has turned into a bar and disco. Food and drink are cheap and most residents can live in more comfortable, if sometimes marooned, conditions then they would in their own country and in weather conditions better than those in northern Europe for at least nine months of the year. Communities of this kind are found all round Menorca and at Cindadela the old capital which has its old fortifications and a Plaza de España and a 14th century Gothic cathedral.

Cindadela is well situated above its harbour and has a more ancient atmosphere than Mahon. There are still traces of the Moorish occupation and influence including some of the old mosque and in the vaulted arches of the narrow streets. As it was once the capital there are numerous fine houses once occupied by the rulers of Menorca and the cathedral and Bishop's palace are in a style appropriate to a centre of power. The cathedral which was founded by Alfonso III soon after the expulsion of the Moors is a formidable looking building built, one might think, as much for defence as worship.

Ibiza

This is the out and out holiday island of the Balearics, a hedonists' paradise dedicated to giving everyone a good time. Brits, French, Germans, Scandinavians, straight, gay or lesbian, all have their niche in Ibiza life. Even Ibizans have a place in the holiday scene as caterers for their visitors though most of them, with a long history of invasion by Romans, Goths, Moors and Barbary pirates, keep their counsel and count the pesetas.

Ibiza town is the centre of the action day and night most of it taking place in the lower town around the harbour and on the Las Salinas and Es Cabellet beaches which are more fashionable than the nearer Figuertas and Talamanca beaches.

The **old town (Dalt Vila)** is on a crag above the sea, its old walls looking like an extension of the cliffs around it. There are three entrances through the walls the Portal de Tablas and the Portal Non admitting motor traffic and the Bastion de San Juan for pedestrians only. The centre of the old town is the **Plaza Desamparados,** the social gathering place where the restaurants and shops are (they stay open until 11 p.m.) are always crowded with tourists in every imaginable form of dress, or undress.

An acknowledgement to culture is made at the Museum de **Arte Comtemporaneo** where modern works of art by artists from all over the world are on exhibition and sale. There is also a Museum Arqueologico with some interesting works of the time of the Carthaginians (7 BC to 3 BC). The ticket to the museum also allows a visit to the Necropolis outside the walls.

Although almost overwhelmed by the tourist tide Ibiza town still has a small fishermen's quarter at Sa Penya, between the harbour and the ramparts where whitewashed houses are piled one above the other and economical bars and restaurants proliferate.

To get around the island one needs a car or a moped, there is a good network of roads but many of the prettier and more secluded coves are at the end of narrow roads. To the north along the east coast from Ibiza town is **Santa Eulalia del Rio** on the estuary of Ibiza's only river. A considerably quieter place than Ibiza with a good beach a few good restaurants and nearby at Ping de Missa on the road to Ibiza town a little medieval fortified town.

Across the island from Ibiza town is **San Antonio Abad,** typical of all the crowded package holiday resorts that Spain has allowed to mushroom along its coasts particularly on the mainland, with high rise hotels, utilitarian restaurants and an undesirable percentage of uncouth visitors.

In recent years Spain seems to have become more aware of what it has lost as a result of the indiscriminate development of tourism but whether it can do anything about it only time will tell.

158

Chapter Eight:
Land of Blood and Love

If you come from a country where the landscape is green and wooded and where rivers flow through rush-bordered banks you may well wonder why Andalucía, the Moorish, Al-Andalus, was regarded as paradise: much of it is dry and rocky, the earth bleached by the sun and supporting only the olive trees which cover mile after square mile of the landscape. Only in the valleys near the rivers that dry up in summer is there lush greenery: oaks, poplars, elms; huge bushes of honeysuckle, bougainvillea and hibiscus; rich crops of cereals, maize, melons, peaches; and the products of market gardens.

Towns and villages are few and far between, lying along the narrow roads like piles of bleached bones scattered along a mountain ridge or a river valley. Once within their boundaries, the contrast is bewitching; the clean white facades of house, or the carved fronts of noble mansions, palm trees, fountains and gardens make any journey across Andalucia worthwhile. Then there are the great cities – Seville, Córdoba, Granada – all retaining the exotic flavour given them by the Moors who turned barren Al Andalus into the paradise of their dreams.

So why is this often barren and ferocious landscape called the land of blood and love? This dates back to the song **Granada** which refers to the bloodshed in reconquering Andalucía and the love of Ferdinand and Isabella for their country and perhaps the love and dalliance of the Moorish courts in their elegant palaces.

☆ ☆ ☆ ☆ ☆

The Moors in Spain

The idea that Spain was totally subject to the Moors from 711 until they were expelled from their kingdom of Granada by Ferdinand and Isabella in 1492 is a simplification of the true events of a complicated medieval period. There was in fact no complete domination by either side and until the time of the Reconquest posession of the Iberian peninsula changed with the different rulers. Throughout the period Spaniards and Moors tolerated each other, did business together and even provided each other with mercenary troops against their own co-religionists.

As the idea of the unification of Spain as a Christians Kingdom took root so the attitudes towards the Moors, and the Jews, who were considered their common allies, hardened and finally brought about the persecution of all those who would not abjure their faith and embrace Catholic Christianity and, also, of those who did so only from expediency.

The Moors, a useful general name for the various Islamic occupiers of Spain, arrived in Spain in 711 under Gib al Tarik (after whom Gibraltar is named). Tarik actually arrived in Algeciras at the instigation of a Visigoth Count Julian who had sworn to avenge his daughters dishonour at the hands of King Rodrigo of the Visigoths or who, more likely, wanted to usurp the throne. The legend of the battle and its aftermath set the tone for the whole history of the Moorish occupation for it tells of prisoners being boiled alive in oil in front of their comrades who were then set free to spread the news of the treatment those who resisted Tarik might expect.

Whether due to this threat or not the Moors found little resistance as they swept through Spain and into France where they were not turned back until Charles Martel defeated them at Poitiers in 732. The Moorish army, then disintegrated and its soldiers dispersed throughout southern France and back into Spain. Those Moors who had been consolidating their gains in Spain also met with some unexpected resistance in the north west where King Pelayo and his mountain guerrillas kept them at bay in Asturias and thus created the springboard from which Spain would eventually be reconquered.

In Spain the seat of Arab power was Córdoba ruled by Abd er Rahman I who had escaped from Damascus after the Abbasid Arabs had ousted and massacred his family, the Ommayids. Abd er Rahman, rallying supporters of the Ommayids in Spain established himself in Córdoba in 756 and with the help of Berber troops soon became the undisputed ruler of Moorish Spain. He ruled by fear and terror during a period in which massacres, decapitations and other forms of mutilation were the fate of all who opposed him. He also however had his more civilised side and founded the great Mosque which is one of the main features of interest in Córdoba today.

As with most dynasties the Ommayid one in Córdoba decayed and a series of ineffective rulers given to hedonistic pleasures allowed the emergence of the powerful warlord Al Mansour, who wreaked havoc in Christian Spain. He sacked Santiago de Compostela and Pamplona in 997 and once again established Moorish authority throughout the peninsula for a brief period.

These military excursions were exercises in intimidation and had little effect on the vast and empty countryside in which castles and walled cities were the strongholds of local feudal lords and their subjects.

When El Mansour died in 1002 the Cordoban influence waned once more while that of the feudal Christian lords of the north became stronger. The greatest of these knights and hero figure who became a symbol of Christian resurgence was El Cid (see Valencia chapter) but his were not the only successful excursions against the Moors. Others successes included those by the Kings of the north; Alfonso I of Aragon who took Zaragoza in 1118, Alfonso VIII of Castile victor of Las Navas de Tolosa in 1212 and Jaime I of Aragon who drove the Moors out the Balearics in 1229 and reconquered Valencia after El Cid's death in 1238.

The slow progress of the Reconquest of Spain is difficult to understand unless you take into account the self interest of the Christians and the Moors who even when they lost or gained territory maintained a tolerant attitude to their conquered people. Both side continued to trade with each other, to employ the labour of the others and to give each other military aid against other feudal lords whether Christian or Moor. There was thus no real incentive to speed up the Reconquest.

By the 15th century however all of Spain except the kingdom of Granada was in Spanish hands and this was soon to become the jewel in the crown of Christian Spain. The country was by this time an amalgam of Visigoth, Moor, Celt, Iberian and Jew all of whom had gradually integrated into the Spanish people but until now there had been no obligation to choose between being a Christian or Moslem or Jew. In an effort to end forever the rivalries between different sections of Spanish society, and to eliminate any threat to national unity a campaign, whose instrument was the Inquisition, began to oblige everyone to give their loyalty to Christian Spain. All those who refused were to be regarded as heretics and all those who were converted for reasons of convenience were also to be persecuted.

The intensification of the campaign of persecution had many justifications among which were: the success of Protestantism in northern Europe and the consequent threat to the Spanish dominions in the Netherlands, Burgundy and Italy, the role of the Jews in financial affairs and their close relationship with the Moors, and the growing maritime threat against the the Spanish American colonies – but above all was the fear of the Islamic powers in the eastern Mediterranean, and North Africa. This took the form of piratical attacks from the Barbary coast and more dangerously, the advance into Europe of Ottoman Turk armies which took Salzburg in 1447, Otranto in 1480 and threatened Naples and Rome. For the Spaniards who, conditioned by the role of Christianity during the Reconquest, saw themselves as the champions of Christian civilisation, the threat of Islam prompted a resolute response. The Spanish believed that Europe was becoming the target for an Islamic pincer movement which would succeed where the Moors had failed: their hunt for potential enemies and traitors therefore became obsessive and led to the systematic erasure of almost all traces of Moorish culture in Spain.

Nevertheless much that is Moorish has survived in the architecture and the way of life and it adds to the experience and enjoyment of all travellers in Andalucia.

☆ ☆ ☆ ☆ ☆

Seville

Seville is a very female city, a woman of the world city, in turns sophisticated and ingenuous, coquettish and practical, beguiling, self-confident, and even a little cynical. She has a dash about her, a bravura that makes her the natural home of Carmen and of Don Juan Tenorio, the model for Mozart's **Don Giovanni.**

If you stand at night near the crossroad of Avenida de la Constitución and Calle Santander with the floodlit fountain at its centre and the lights of cars passing like shooting stars up the dark avenues where horse-drawn carriages ignore the motorised hub-bub, you receive one impression of the life of Seville; if you stroll down the lamplit street of the Barrio Santa Cruz you gain another. Across the Canal Alfonso XIII, once the course of the now diverted River Guadalquivir, it is different again, though Triana is not the working class and gipsy quarter it once was. During the day the pedestrian shopping precinct around Calle Sierpes and the business quarter at its western end is as busy and lively as any similar centre of a modern city. For the visitors, the real

163

Andálucia

Linares

Ubeda

Baeza

Granada

Jaén

Antequera

Córdoba

Ecija

Ronda

Carmona

Arcos de la Frontera

Seville

Jerez de la Frontera

Cadiz

centre of Seville is the area around the great brooding mass of the cathedral which sits where the mosque of the Almohades Moors, who also built the elegant Giralda Tower, once stood.

By great good fortune Seville, unlike other cities of Spain, has retained many aspects of its long and dramatic life, not as museum pieces, islands in a sea of modern concrete, but as parts of the living city.

This makes her a superb city to get to know, not in a brief encounter, but in a visit without counting the time.

● Around the Giralda and the Cathedral

The **Giralda Tower,** visible from most parts of Seville and once topped by goldern globes that flashed in the sun for travellers to see 20 miles away, is the symbol of Seville. Tall, elegant, with her impeccable brickwork topped with a turret of gleaming tiles. From the top, reached by a spiral gradient, there is a magnificent view of the city called Isbeya by the Moors, of which the Giralda is the only notable remainder.

After Seville was captured from the Moors by Ferdinand III of Castile and Leon in 1278 the mosque which stood alongside the tower was used as a Christian church for a time. But with the growing intolerance of the 'Reconquista', this could not be tolerated and the mosque was destroyed, though, strangely, the tower was spared.

In place of the mosque the present **Cathedral of Santa María** was built in the 15th century, a fortress of a building hovering between a Gothic and Renaissance style and of an extraordinary sense of power. There are nine portals to the cathedral all of them with notable features. The main door Puerta Mayor is flanked by the Door of the Baptism (**Puerta del Bautismo**) and the Door of the Birth (**Puerta del Nacimiento**.

The contrast between the bright daylight outside and the gloom within is temporarily confusing but soon the light filtering through the 16th-century stained glass windows high on the cathdral walls reveals the interior. Soaring fluted colums set out evenly around a huge central stone block contain the choir: almost a church within a church. Around

165

the perimeter of the vast space are the chapels and at the eastern end is the high altar, set apart from the choir by a huge metal gilded screen and dominated by its enormous reredos, 37 m (120 ft) high and crowded with gilded carved figures. Behind the altar the Royal Chapel (**Capilla Real**) contains the tombs of Ferdinand III (later canonised), and Pedro the Cruel of Castile, whose daughters married the sons of John of Gaunt and who helped make Seville into a great city in its post-Moorish years. For most visitors, these founders of Spain are probably less interesting than Christopher Columbus, whose tomb lies in the southern aisle of the cathedral. This monument is a 19th century tribute to the discoverer of America, in whom his royal masters lost interst and who died in poverty. His body was first buried in Valladolid, then removed to Santo Domingo in the West Indies, then to Havana and finally returned to Spain in 1899 after Cuban independence. Today it lies in a casket carried with pomp and circumstance by four figures representing Castile, Leon, Navarre and Aragon.

A relic of the original mosque remains in the Courtyard of the Oranges (**Patio de las Naranjas**) on the north side of the cathedral. Here there is a Moorish fountain round which orange trees still grow. A curiosity of the courtyard is the stuffed crocodile hanging at the Gate of the Lizard.

The cathedral well reflects the importance and wealth of Seville after the discovery of America, the story of which extraordinary enterprise is contained in the nearby Archives of the Indies (**Archivo de las Indies**), which also houses documents tracing the subsequent history of Spanish America. The Archives started life as a Commercial Exchange, designed by Juan de Herrera who also built the Escorial for Philip II, and became an archive when the great days of Spanish trade with the Americas was over.

● The Alcazar

The most surprising and undoubtedly most wonderful building to be found near Seville Cathedral is the Alcázar which lies behind a modest castellated wall in the Plaza del Triumfo to the south of the cathedral. The Royal Palace (**Alcázar or Ataranzas Reales**) is in the Moorish style, though it was largely built for Pedro the Cruel who, although a Christian, preferred the company of the Moors and their style of life. You enter the palace through a luxuriant green courtyard, where there are usually a few stray kittens, and the original Moorish outer wall to come into the Patio de la Montera, dominated by the elegant facade of Pedro the Cruel's Palace.

Inside, the elaborate and delicate stucco work rivals that of the Alhambra and if you have ever felt that all this swirling abstract design is not for you, prepare to be instantly converted. The work is Mudejar, that is, by Moors in Christian-held territories, and it is a miracle that it has lasted six centuries considering that its decorations are only plasterwork on a brick foundation. Among the outstanding parts of the building are the Court of the Maidens (**Patio de las Doncellas**), the Court of the Dolls (**Patio de Las Muñecas**), where Pedro the Cruel is said to have assassinated his brother in one of those dynastic quarrels so common in medieval times, and the Hall of the Ambassadors (**Salon de los Embajadores**) which has a superb coffered cupola topped by a lantern.

The Moors had a trick of creating a sense of infinity in the smallest places by opening doorways and pillared porticos in all rooms, designed to lead the eye down long vistas of decorated spaces to produce a sense of peace and a feeling of eternity – an effect sometimes difficult to experience today when the rooms are full of tourists.

You do not get the same feeling in the addition to the palace called the Contracts Chamber (**Casa de Contratación**) which was built by Isabella off the entrance courtyard. This large, tall room with a wooden beamed ceiling was intended as a clearing house for commercial deals concerning Spanish America, a point which is underlined by the board room table that today occupies a part of it.

After the Conquistadors came the royal administrators, businessmen and civil servants; no doubt, many negotiations and much nepotism, bribery and business corruption took place round the table in the Contracts Chamber. Both

Isabella and Ferdinand presided over meetings here, and probably walked in the lovely gardens that lie to the south of the palace.

● Barrio Santa Cruz

The **Barrio Santa Cruz,** lying to the north east of the Alcázar, is a carefully preserved and well-maintained village of white-washed houses, narrow streets and squares full of the sight and scent of geraniums, honeysuckle, bougainvillea and other flowers. Until 1492, when the Spanish Kings expelled unconverted Jews as well as Moslems from their lands, this was a Jewish quarter. Today it is a delightful imaginary world of Sevillian romance, and of fashionable little houses. At night, large lamps light the streets well and people walk around in it safely. It is a good place for restaurants where you may eat in a square under the stars and listen to some rather bad flamenco singing but nevertheless enjoy yourself. The Square of the Venerable Priests (**Plaza de los Venerables Sacerdotes**) has three such restaurants and while you eat cats slink about in dark corners, well-behaved little dogs look up at you hopefully and children play catch in the alleys.

On the edges of the Santa Cruz area are many of those small bars where the youth of Spain like to congregate between 8 pm and 10 pm, spilling out into the narrow streets where they stand, sit on the pavement or perch on their motorbikes and talk. Boys and girls gazing into each others eyes and exchanging mostly chaste kisses, obediently separating at the curfew time set by their parents.

Less well preserved and with larger buildings, though no less narrow streets, is the quarter west of Santa Cruz to the south of Calle Menendez Pelayo which marks the perimeter of the old city wall. Here there are surprises at every turning, old churches, the house of Pilate (**Casa de Pilatos**) said to be a replica of the Roman Governor's in Jerusalem, and the ruined column of a Roman Temple among them.

● Sierpes

The Avenida de la Constitucion which runs south of the cathedral leads to the Square of San Francisco (Plaza de San Francisco) and the classical Town Hall (**Ayuntamiento**) whose surface is rich in plateresque decorations. At its northern end begins the traffic-free Sierpes Street (Calle de los Sierpes) and adjoining streets. There are some attractive old shopfronts in polished wood as well as smart modern windows along here. In some stretches thoughtful shopkeepers have put awnings across the street – against the hot sun rather than rain, one imagines. Sierpes leads into the modern centre of Seville. Also in this quarter are some popular 'tapas' bars such as the Salvador, named after the nearby church.

● Parque Maria Lusia

If you have a nostalgia for old Seville be a tourist and go to the **Parque Maria Luisa** in a horse-drawn coach – no longer the old hacks that used to ply the streets, but carriages fit for an **hidalgo.** The best time is after sunset. The park has a rich variety of trees, including elms, palms, eucalyptus and magnolias, and contains many buildings built for the 1929 Hispano American exhibition. The centre piece is the huge **Plaza de España,** built in a Mudéjar style with two tall towers at each end of the semi-circular palace which embraces the Plaza. There is a fountain (lit at night) here and a canal navigable by small boats.

Noteworthy buildings are the **Lope de Vega Theatre,** and the buildings housing the **Museum of Popular Art** and the **Archaelogical Museum.** In the theatre are performed some of the plays of Lope de Vega (1562-1635), a successful dramatist who served in the Armada and gave most of his money to charity and of Calderon de la Barea (1600-1681), a soldier and court dramatist to Philip IX. In the Museum of Popular Art, you may see some of the accessories of Seville's Holy week and learn about its history, though the stars of Holy Week, the saints and virgins whose effigies are paraded through the streets, are kept in the churches. The Archaeological Museum has a collection of archaeological relics found in the region, in particular a fine Roman torso, said to be Hadrian, and a beautiful head of a girl which looks suprisingly modern.

● Triana

Across the old River Guadalquivir deflected round the city in the 1920s leaving its old course dammed and now called the Canal Alfonso XIII, is the **Triana** quarter. This was once the home of the Seville gipsies, an area of narrow, poverty-stricken streets and the sad sounds of **Canto Hondo,** but no longer. The old quarter is now surrounded by a modern city and the Calle Pages del Corro, bordering its western edge, is full of show rooms displaying the cars that have become a status symbol in modern Spain, greater than the smart clothes, expensive shoes and gold jewellery of yesteryear.

Some of Triana's old streets still survive between the river and the Pages del Corro; there are bars and gipsies and, if the mood is right and the guitarists and singers with **duende** are around, you may hear that haunting sound of the **Canto hondo.** But, as a young man with dark brooding look of a gipsy told me, 'it doesn't happen often now'. **Duende,** about which the poet Federico Garcia Lorca wrote, and which he possessed, is that quality that makes and raises art above technique or craftsmanship. **Duende** is something that comes from the soul, whatever that is, and all great art has it. It is something that transforms the simplest phrase into magic.

If you do not find **duende** in Triana do not despair; instead, go to the Rio Grande restaurant by the Puente San Telmo. This restaurant, though what one might call an upmarket tourist eating place, has a good menu and fine wines but its greatest asset is that it looks across the canal to the city. At night, with the floodlit Giraldo Tower and Golden Tower (**Torre de Oro**) which was once covered in gold tiles, the river is magical. If you eat late you will see the lights gradually dim, the two cruise boats which started off earlier in the evening will be berthed, the traffic across the bridge will diminish and from the dark waters you may get a whisper of the **duende** of old Seville.

Flamenco has not entirely disappeared from the night life of Seville and there are several places where you can enjoy the whirling layered skirts, the stamping feet and rattling castanets of gipsy shows. Some of these are near the Maestranza building by the river to the west of the cathedral area.

Along the Guadalquivir

Around Seville the land is flat and divided into a cubist pattern of quadrilateral fields. This the land of **regadío,** of agriculture made possible by the irrigation of the yellow ochre earth so that the orchards and melon patches provide juicy, sun-ripened fruit.

Once, the river here was crowded with barges carrying away the produce of the land which the Moors had cultivated; today, the fruits and vegetables are transported on juggernauts that thunder along the road to Madrid, some taking the lower river road and other the higher road to the south along the route to Carmona and Ecija.

Carmona, the first town to the east of Seville bursts into view in a blinding flash of white cubes piled one on top of the other. In this world of utter whiteness it is almost a relief to see the grey, dusty pavements and the soberly dressed people trudging along the streets: an old lady in grey, her hair pulled back to a tight bun, arguing the price of a lettuce under a tattered parasol; a man on an ancient bicycle whose carrier is piled with empty boxes; a mother berating her child; men waiting on corners and near bars – for what?

Carmona as a town is very aware of Seville only 33 km (20 miles) away, so it grooms itself carefully. There is a handsome, carefully maintained church here and several fine houses but the crowning glory of Carmona is the castle, squat as a bullfrog astride the upper end of the main street. The castle, in what was Pedro the Cruel's favourite town, was rebuilt by Ferdinand and Isabella and is now the splendid **Parador Alcázar del Rey Don Pedro** which has a splendid Mudeja-style patio and a modern swimming pool.

The town also has several churches worthy of a visit, especially **Santa María la Mayor** which, though in Spain

171

Renaissance and Baroque style, contains remains of the former mosque whose site it occupies.

Also not to be missed in Carmona is the **Roman Necropolis.** Because of its position above the Guadalquivir Valley the Romans considered the town of great strategic importance. Scipio Africanus defeated Hasdrubal the Carthaginian here in 206 BC, and there was large armed camp at Carmona for some time. The necropolis is one of the largest in Spain, containing at least 1,000 graves and tombs sheltering the ashes or bodies of Romans and mercenaries who served the Empire. A reminder of the Carthaginian use elephants as a kind of living military tank is in the painting of one of these splendid African creatures of the tomb called the Triclinio del Elefante.

Eastwards from Carmona the landscape becomes dryer and rockier, with long vistas of undulating hills through which the metalled road takes you to **Ecija,** know as el Sartén de España (the Spanish frying pan). Its reputation for scorching summer heat is not more deserved here than in other places in Andalucía but it has stuck to Ecija, which prefers to be remembered for its many baroque towers.

Ecija, called Astigi by the Romans, is a pretty town and has the remains of a Moorish fortress. Its long main street, the Calle de los Caballeros, has many fine old houses, all well maintained and dazzling white. The famous towers in the Mudéjar style with brickworks and azulejos were mostly rebuilt in the 18th century after an earthquake and some of them alongside ruined churches. Among towers to look for are the parish church of St James (**Santiago el Mayor**), Santa Cruz and Santa Maria whose style imitates that of the Giralda in Seville. The Palacio de los Marqueses de Peñaflor (**Palace of the Peñaflor Marquees**) with its painted facade and baroque doorway, is the most impressive of the large mansions.

Córdoba

After Ecija there is little of note along the Guadalquivir valley until **Córdoba.** The city on the Guadalquiver, cultural centre of the Moors, comes into view suddenly as the road breasts a spur of hill. The first view is disappointing for Córdoba today is a thriving industrial town but, once in the city, industry is soon forgotten. Like most of the cities and towns of Andálucia, which corresponds to the Roman Baetica, Córdoba has its roots in Roman and Moorish culture. Among the great Romans born here were Seneca the elder and younger (the latter was Nero's tutor), and Lucanus, a nephew of the younger Seneca who, having outstripped Nero in a poetry contest, became his enemy and a conspirator against the tyrant. The conspiracy being discovered, Lucanus took his life in the Roman manner by cutting his veins in his bath.

When the Moors displaced the Visigoths who had followed the Romans, Córdoba became the centre of Moorish Spain under Abd er Rahman I, II and III, becoming finally a Caliphate independent of the nominal capital of Damascus. As in other parts of Spain, the Moors introduced agriculture, setting up vast irrigation systems to make the best use of the waters of the Guadalquivir; they developed the leather industry for which Cordoba is still famous, and they set up schools, universities, mosques, hospitals and public baths. The cultural influence of Cordoba on Europe was considerable and its learned men, like Averroes, who introduced the work of Aristotle to the west, and Maimonides, a Jewish Aristotelian and doctor of medicine, spread the ideas that brought Europe from the Dark Ages into the Renaissance. The Cordoban caliphate, which had been so successful under the Omayyad rulers, eventually decayed in the 11th century and the centre of Moorish culture moved to Seville.

● The old Moorish quarter

Cordoba is a fine example of the tolerant communities that existed in Spain before the coming of the Catholic monarchs and the Inquisition, and old Cordoba can still show part of both Moorish and Jewish quarters.

The area stretches from the pier between the New Bridge (**Puente Nuevo**) and Puente Romano and the broad, tree-filled boulevard of the Avenida del Conde de Vallecano and its continuation, the Paseo Este de la Victoria.

The dominant feature of the quarter is the **Mosque (La Mezquita),** built by Abd er Rahman I and added to later by Abd er Rahman II and Al Mansur. Though converted to Christian use in 1236, the mosque remained intact until another purely Christian edifice was built inside it. The mosque character of the building as a whole remains dominant, however.

The ground area of the mosque is vast: 185 metres (600 ft) by 132 metres (430 ft) and the profusion of columns and arches, with the sense of infinity that they engender, makes it seem even larger.

Though there are several gates through the surrounding castellated wall into the mosque, today only one, the Gate of Pardons (**Puerta del Perdon**) is used. The original Moorish gate is St Stephens Gate (**Puerta de San Esteban**) on the west side).

The Puerta de las Palmas is the entrance from the Patio de los Naranjos into the mosque itself, through the wall built by Christians. Before this, the courtyard side of the mosque had been open, thus allowing in more light than there is today in the dim interior.

Unlike Christian churches, the Córdoba Mezquita has an unregimented space, without specific areas designed for particular functions. It is simply a space designed for prayer and meditation. The effect is rather like being in a forest: columns rise on all sides, forming arches through which one sees other colums and more arches and colums ad infinitum. The colums have carved capitals and the arches are decorated with red and white marble stripes. If there is a focal point in the Mosque it is the mihrab on the south wall, a beautiful octagonal domed space with moorish decorations which indicated the direction of the holy city of Mecca.

The Christian parts of the mosque lie in the centre. Here are a choir transept and Chapel Royal (**Capilla Mayor**). These were built in the 16th century in an ornate style which, according to legend, even Charles V objected to, though the Capilla Mayor with its Mudéjar decoration harmonises with the mosque well enough.

Near the mosque, by the river is all that remains of the Moorish **Alcázar (Palace) and Alcazaba.** The largest remnant of the fortress is the Torre de la Calahorra which is now a museum of city archives, including momentoes of Gonzalez de Córdoba, El Gran Capitan, the miltary leader who was responsible for the capture of the Kingdom of Naples in 1495, during the reign of the Catholic monarchs, Isabella and Ferdinand.

The Alcázar was rebuilt by Alfonso XI in the 14th century, though echocs of the original moorish palace remain in the patios and in the superb riverside gardens which combine ponds, fountains and flowers in a way that reminds one of the Generallife in Granada. The gardens are illuminated until midnight and provide a romantic place to walk in the evenings. Perhaps the last Moorish King of Granada, Boabdil, who was kept imprisoned in Cordoba, walked here musing on the destruction of Moorish Spain. Columbus, who saw Ferdinand and Isabella here before setting off on his first voyage, must have meditated and wondered what lay in store for him.

To the north of the Moorish buildings lies the **Judería,** the old Jewish quarter, a place of narrow streets and white-washed houses; no doubt its inhabitants in the 15th and 16th centuries walked in fear and trembling for the Inquisition had one of its headquarters in the nearby Alcázar. The old synagogue still exists in Calle de Maimonides, a Mudéjar building built in 1315 but now hardly more than a shell. In the Judería by the old city walls is the Municipal museum **(Museo Municipal Taurino)** with a bullfight exhibition including mementoes of famous Cordoban 'Manolete', who was killed at nearby Linares, and of El Cordobés.

When the Christians took over in Cordoba they made it their town, building churches like **San Lorenzo (St Laurence)** whose tower was originally a minaret, and palaces like the **Palacio de Marques de Viana** which is the Córdoba Archaeological Museum, one of the most important in Andalucía.

To the north of the Palacio Paez lies the Plaza de las Tendillas, the centre of the 19th-century town whose tall, dignified houses, complete with wrought-iron balconies, have a Victorian air. Though Plaza de las Tendillas is a busy place with commerical houses and shops in the surrounding streets it lacks the symmetry of the traditional Plaza Mayor of most Spanish cities. You will find this style of square at the Plaza della Corredera, a fine but neglected square where bull fights once took place and which is now the site of a market, whose stalls occupy the paved centre. Another pretty square with the patina of age on its buildings is the Colt Square (**Plaza del Potro**), once a livestock market, a fact which the prancing horse on its fountain indicates. Cervantes once stayed at the inn on the plaza which faces the former charity hospital, now home to a collection of the works of the painter Julio Romero de Torres whose romanticised paintings of dark-eyed, dark-skinned Spanish ladies became a 19-century cliché. In another part of the building are paintings by artists of an earlier Cordoban school and by other Spanish painters such as Goya, Ribera, Murillo and Zurbaran.

Medina Azahara

Eight kilometres (5 miles) outside Córdoba lie the ruins of what may well have been the real capital of the Omayyad moors. According to legend, Medina Azahara was built by Abd er Rahman III for his beautiful wife, Zoraida. It is known that the royal family lived here for a quarter of a century and that around the palace, remains of which are visible today and more is being excavated a city of some 12,000 inhabitants grew up. The reconstructed remains of the palace, built at the top of a series of terraces, show splendid rooms with horseshoe arches supported by columns with carved capitals.

Remains of stucco work, paintings and carvings give an impression of the palace's former glory. It may have been this luxury which prompted a revolt by Berber Arabs in, who attacked and destroyed the buildings; after that the palace was looted and used as quarry for stone for other buildings so that little of it now remains.

Cordoban fiestas

The Andalucian cities all have spectacular festivals in springtime, most of them related to religious festivals, though their origins may well be pagan. In Córdoba, the May and Autumn festivals provide an opportunity for the same kind of jamboree as the one that takes place in Holy Week in Seville. There are processions, parades of Cordoban horses and bullfights, with many people taking the opportunity to wear Andalucian dress, the girls in dresses with layered skirts and the men in the Cordoban country style with the flat felt hats, waistcoats, leather chaps and short riding boots that became the style of ranch men all over the Americas.

The upper reaches of the Quadalquivir

The Guadalquivir flows across the north of Andalucía along the foothills of the Sierra Morena which rises like a wall between the last kingdom of the Moors and New Castile. In its upper reaches it has little water except during the period of the melting snows of springtime and it supports little agriculture. The land through which it flows is hilly, an ocean of a territory with long heaving vistas of hills and rocky outcrops and endless rows of olive trees standing out like puffs of smoke on the white, bleached earth.

Among these acres of olives and hills lie two of the most magnificent small towns of Andalucía. One of these, on the N 322 that leads through the empty landscape of Almería to Valenica, is **Ubeda**; the other, off this highway, is **Baeza**.

● Ubeda

Ubeda has had the good fortune – or good sense – to preserve its old town almost intact inside the semicircle of the Cava Rastro along which ran the old city wall. Modern Ubeda is much like other Spanish towns, with tall 18th and 19th-century houses, squares with trees and monuments and the Plaza de Toros. But if you take the Calle Real, just behind the stone tower of the police station which has always been the headquarters of the town law and order according

177

to the officer on duty, you soon find yourself in a different world.

Calle Real was evidently a popular shopping street at one time, though it is being deserted for the now fashionable streets of the modern town. It retains buildings from its greater days, however. Ubeda's rich citizens favoured the Renaissance style, as evidenced by two fine buildings in honey-coloured stone along the Calle Real. The larger of them is the Palacio Vela de los Cibos, which stands on the corner of a square which itself leads on to the Plaza Vasquez de Molina and another spendid array of Renaissance and Baroque buildings over-looking grassy plots with trees. The **Casa de las Cadenas,** so called for the chains that border its courtyard, faces across to the elegantly ornate church of Santa Maria and, in a long rectangle leading of the Plaza Vasquez, is the Renaissance church of San Salvador, the decorated facade of which looks like an elaborate stage set, and whose interior includes a flamboyant reredos by Berruguete and an elegant sacristy. The church was built by Molina, secretary to Charles V, and has remained in the family ever since as a private chapel. In this handsome tree-bordered square is a fine parador, the **Parador Nacional del Condestable Dávalos,** set in the former Palacio de last Ortegas, an elegant and restrained two-storey Renaissance building with an attractive inner courtyard complete with colonnade and plants in giant earthenware jars. The paradors bar, restaurant, and rooms are charming and beautifully furnished.

Alongside the parador is the Hogar de Pensionistas (old people's home) where you may see Ubeda's pensioners enjoying social get togethers, eating, drinking, playing cards, all with great animation and providing lively evidence of the improved welfare facilities available in modern Spain.

Around this are numerous narrow streets with immaculate white-washed houses and large stone mansions, among which are the **Tower Mansion (Casa de las Torres)** and the **Savages' house (Casa de los Salvages),** on whose facade two wild and hairy creatures, naked and chained, hold the owner's coat of arms. The wild savages are, probably, wretched natives of the South American colonies which provided so much of the revenue squandered by successive Spanish governments from the time of Charles V onwards.

A day could easily be spent at Ubeda discovering its delights; one such would be the handsome Romanesque/Gothic church of St Paul (**San Pablo**) on the shaded Plaza 1° de Mayo.

● Baeza

Baeza, only a few miles from Ubeda, has kept its old town perfectly preserved within a ring road, following the line of the old city walls from which there is a spectacular view of hills and olive trees heaving and humping away towards the horizon like a tumultous ocean.

The main way into the old town is through the **Plaza del Populo,** also called the Lion Square or Plaza de los Leones because of its fountain with lions, and a stone archway called the Arco de Jaén. From here, you must choose between continuing round the ramparts or climbing into the town up a steep road leading to the Santa Cruza Square (Plaza Santa Cruz) where there is a small Romanesque church and the **Palacio de Jabalquinto,** a lovely palace with an admirable Isabelline facade and a fine courtyard overlooked by a splendid balcony at present being restored.

A long sloping street with attractive buildings, including a school from which children pour out at one o'clock to find their neatly dressed mothers waiting on the pavement, stretches up towards the large, cobbled Plaza de Santa María, with a fountain at the centre and the Casas Consistoriales stretching out below it with the arms of Juana the Mad and Philip the Handsome on the first floor facade.

As in Ubeda, there is a wealth of buildings to enjoy at old Baeza, which has been so zealously protected from commercial developments that you will have to go outside the walls to the long rectangular arcaded Plaza de la Constitución for refreshments.

There are cafés at intervals all the way round the Plaza. At its side, nearest the Plaza del Populo, are two in sharp contrast; one has juke boxes, television and all the paraphernalia of contemporary bars, and the other is a clean, quiet place offering a variety of sandwiches and is run by a painter whose work hangs round the walls and whose favourite subjects are Baeza and, in particular, the olive trees of his native land.

The poet, Antonio Machado, who spent some years in Baeza eking out a living as a teacher, after the death of his wife had almost driven him to suicide, thought that Baeza was a philistine place, but the evidence of the old town raises the thought that this was not always so.

● Jaén

Two great hills dominate the city of **Jaén.** On one stands the **Castle of Santa Catalina** and on the other the **Cathedral of Santa Maria.** Between them, on the lower slopes, lies the town, rebuilt largely in the past hundred years and a busy, commercial place of large modern blocks among which flow non-stop streams of traffic controlled by frantic policemen with much blowing of whistles and waving of arms.

The old part of the city lies on a hill and dominated by the massive cathedral with its two towers and dome built by the ubiquitous architect Andres de Vandelvira in the 16th century. The facade is imposing and combines Renaissance and Baroque characterisation; the interior is equally grand and has a fine, well-carved choir stall as well as many chapels with various interesting works. Within the building is a museum devoted to the history of Jaen Cathedral.

In front of the cathedral is a large paved terrace with trees where families gather in the evenings, their children free to run about, play football, ride bicycles and generally let off steam. Younger people tend to collect at the small bars in the narrow winding streets around the cathedral. There are not many of these, however, nor, as one might expect in the picturesque old quarter, many restaurants. The reason is that Jaén is not a tourist town and remains, according to one young lady resident, a very quiet place.

Since the days of its reconquest by Ferdinand III (the Saint) in 1246 Jaen has been a crossroad for travellers from Andalucía to Castile. Proof of its strategic importance is visible in the powerful castle on the crest of Santa Catalina hill. This fortress, held by the Moors and improved later by the Christians, is now a parador (temporarily closed) and has one of the finest views in Andalucía, looking out south over the city and the olive-covered hills to the Sierra Nevada and to the north to the barrier of the Sierra Morena, once a natural defence of the Andalucian Moorish kingdom and entered only by the Pass of Despeñaperros, which, roughly translated, means 'the Pass where the Moorish dogs are hurled off the rocks'.

Granada

In their retreat down Spain the Moors were cornered in Andalucia or 'Al-andalus', as they called it. Then they were driven from Cordoba to Seville and finally to their mountain kingdom of **Granada.**

The town, called 'Carnata' by the Moors, became their headquarters in 1236 after the fall of Cordoba. Here they survived – in some luxury – until 1492 when Ferdinand and Isabella set their hearts on conquering this last piece of Moorish Spain. The rulers of Granada were the Nasrids under whom the city, filled with artists, craftsmen and the businessmen fleeing from the Christian takeovers of their cities, flourished. At the time there was still a certain tolerance for the Moorish kingdom and, indeed, for the talented Moors but internal dissension among the Moorish families of Granada brought about their downfall. According to legend, the roots of the dispute went back to the time when the Caliph Muley Abur Hassan had fallen in love with a Christian girl and had exiled his queen Aicha and her son Boabdil. They eventually returned to drive out the Caliph, setting Boabdil on the throne. Unfortunately, in a skirmish with the Christians Boabdil was captured and only released under conditions which the powerful family of the Abencerrajes believed to be against Moorish interests. Suspecting a plot against him, Boabdil arranged to have 36 members of the Abencerrajes murdered at a banquet given in the Alhambra: a brutal way to deal with his problem, no doubt, but a not unusual solution in the Middle Ages. The political

disarray among the Moors played into the hands of Ferdinand and Isabella and Granada was taken on 2 January,
1492, the same year that Columbus discovered America (on
October 12). In truth, the Moors of Granada had been
collaborating with the Christian Spaniards for some time,
even helping them to capture other Moorish towns in
dubious horse-trading to secure their own survivial.

In Granada the Moors left behind them evidence of a
highly civilised culture, which arouses our speculation as to
what Spain might have become if Arab and Christian co-
operation had not succumbed to the demands and pressures
of the world of the Catholic Monarchs, Philip II and Charles
V.

● The Alhambra

If architecture personifies the character of the culture that
engenders it, then the buildings of **the Alhambra** provide
much to meditate upon. There are three main blocks on the
spur of hill above the modern town: the Alcazaba fortress,
built in the 9th century; the Alhambra palace, largely erected
by the Nasrid caliphs Yusuf I (1333-54) and Mohammed V
(1354-91); and the palace of Charles V, built in the 16th
century. The Alcazaba is simply a blunt military statement,
its walls, towers, parade ground and soldiers' quarters
designed to defy all challengers and inspire fear in any
would-be attackers. The other two are different, each
reflecting the ethos of their builders. The Moorish palace has
the refinement of people who appreciated the subtle harmo-
nies of proportion, and the delicate understatement of
intricate geometrical designs: though perhaps it also reflects
a decaying culture which has succumbed to the temptations
of the flesh and intellectual dalliance. Charles V's palace, in
contrast, speaks of power and authority; it is the building of a
culture committed to dominance and to progress through a
powerful centralised system of government. In the Moorish
buildings, an almost feminine sensibility is demonstrated in
the arcades with their fine columns, the fountains, the lace-
like tracery of the decorative plasterwork, all delicately
combining like chamber music; in the palace of Charles V the

massive stone blocks of the tower facade, the solid Doric
colums of the circular court, the heavy pediments of the first
floor windows sound a Wagnerian note.

● The Moorish Palace

The palace consists of a series of courtyards from which the
visitor steps into the series of small, exquisitely decorated
rooms around them. The first of these courts is the **Patio del
Mexuar,** a small tall-sided court in lucent white marble with
two elegant facades, one with an arcade leading into the
Golden Room and the other, opposite it, a simple but
exquisitely proportioned wall leading into the main palace.

The largest of the courts, **Court of the Myrtles (Patio de los
Arrayanes)** is also beautifully simple and totally enchanting.
A long rectangular pond bordered by a low-clipped bed of
myrtles has at one end an elegant colonnade with decorated
arches behind which rises one of the formidable towers of the
outer defences of the Alhambra. At the other end there is an
additional storey with rounded windows above which rises a
gallery roofed with red tiles. Behind this looms a part of
Charles V's heavy Renaissance palace.

The third major court is the **Lion Court (Patio de los
Leones),** where a friendly group of lions looking like Great
Dane pups spout water while supporting on their backs a
large stone fountain. The Patio de los Leones, the most
elaborate of the courts, is surrounded by an arcade with
fragile-looking paired and single colums and decorated
arches. At either end is a pavilion supported on more
columns and on the other walls there are entrances to other
rooms and galleries. In one of these, the **Hall of Abencerrajes,** Boabdil arranged the massacre of the Abencerrajes.

On the opposite side of the Patio de los Leones a doorway
leads into other rooms of the palace, including those used by
Charles V, who perhaps found solace here away from the
overbearing magnificence of his own palace.

From the palace you can wander into other green courts,
the **Patio Lindaraja,** and the **Gardens of Partal (Jardines del
Partal)** and so along the protecting walls and towers to the
Generalife.

In such a brief description of this lovely and touching royal building it is impossible to do it justice, to describe the intricacy of the gesso work, the decorative calligraphy of the lines of poetry woven into the designs that cover the walls, the feminine sensibility of the whole place. Perhaps it was the fact that the palace marked the end of the Moors' residence in Spain that gives it such poignancy. This was the dying note of a seven-centuries-long occupation during which time the Moors had brought agriculture, science, mathematics and philosophy to a Europe of feudal ignorance and brutality. It is appropriate that the Moorish swansong should have been expressed in such fragile material as wood, ceramics and gesso. The wonder is that it has survived until today.

● The Palace of Charles V

If the patio of the Moorish Alhambra seems to echo to the sounds of poetry and stringed instruments, then the grand circular central court of Charles V palace resounds with the clatter of horses' hooves and the clash of armour. The court, like the palace designed by Pedro Machuca of Toledo who had studied in Italy, has all the grandeur and aggressiveness that characterised the growth of the great powers of Europe throughout the 16th, 17th, 18th and 19th centuries.

Charles V was the most powerful monarch of his age, ruler of Austria, Germany, Burgundy, the Netherlands, Spain and Spanish America. He was also a slave to the demands of his dominions and to the factions from the rival powers of France and the increasing challenge of Tudor England.

The palace, intended as an expression of Hapsburg power in the same way as cathedrals were symbols of Papal power, was never completed in Charles V's time. The Moors who were forced to pay for its construction rebelled and the work was discontinued.

Today, the palace contains two museums, one of Hispano Moorish objects (**the Museo Nacional de Arte Hispano Arabe**) including sculptures and ceramics and the other a fine arts museum (**Museo Provincial de Bellas Artes**) with paintings of the 16th to 18th century.

● The Generalife

Across a valley above the walls of the Alhambra on the slopes of the Hill of the Sun (**Cerro del Sol**) lies an intimate and peaceful retreat filled with the sound of fountains and the smell of roses and honeysuckle. This is the **Generalife,** the country house of the Moorish Kings of Granada. To understand how three or four rectangular enclosed gardens should possess such a magical atmosphere, you must go there. Most of the present buildings are reconstructions of the Moorish houses, complete with their columns and arches, but the layout of the gardens is much as the Moors knew them. In the two main gardens, the Court of the canal (**Patio de la Acequia**) and the Court of the Fountains (**Patio de los Surtidores**) fine streams of water leap into the air falling like rain on hot sunlit pools. Roses, oleanders, geraniums, jasmine and many other flowers grow in wild profusion among arches of fir trees which also line the hill above the Generalife. A solitary cypress marks the trysting place where Boadbdil's wife met her Abencerrajes lover and perhaps gave her husband another reason for getting rid of his enemies.

● Downtown Granada

From the terrace of the Alhambra Palace Hotel, a delightful imitation Alhambra on the wooded slopes, the trees of which were planted on the order of the Duke of Wellington, there is a splendid view of Granada. To the left lie the high mountains of the Sierra Nevada, below is the Church of Saint Cecilia, in the middle distance the spires of the Virgen de las Angustias, to the right the tiled dome of Saint Dominic's and far over to the right, just in view, the Cathedral of Santa Maria de La Encarnacion.

Across the city, though not distinguishable among the jumble of houses, is the Avenue of the Catholic Monarchs (**Avenida de los Reyes Catolicos**) under which flows the Darro River which disappears from sight at the Plaza Santa Ana between the Alhambra and the Albaicin Gipsy quarter. Like Triana in Seville, this is not what it once was, though you can

185

enjoy (if that is the word) some of its atmosphere by eating at El Ladrillo, a fish restaurant, if you do not mind being importuned by gipsies. Better still, if the gipsy legend interests you go to Sacromonte, beyond the Albaicin, where you can visit them in their well-appointed caves. Most parts of the city are within walking distance of the Avenida de los Reyes Catolicos.

● Around the Cathedral

A focal point of the centre of the city of Granada is the statue of a seated Isabella receiving Christopher Columbus, a Genoese, at the junction of Gran Via de Colon with Reyes Católicos. High on their pedestal, the two figures play the roles given to them by a sentimental 19th century who forgot that Columbus hardly received any thanks for his daring voyage and died forgotten. Behind them, a glass and concrete bank building symbolises the commercial enterprise of the new post-Franco EEC Spain. Around them the cars whirl, sound their horns and make the pedestrians look sharp.

Facing the statue is the spiritual and social centre of the city, around the great mass of the **Catedral de Santa María de la Encarnación** and the Royal Chapel (**Capillá Real**). The cathedral built by, among others, Diego de Silva, in the 16th century is in an imposing Renaissance style derived from St Peter's in Rome. The facade, which has one solid square tower, was designed by Alonso Cano.

The interior is imposing. There is a fine chancel with Corinthian columns and several gilded chapels, such as that of Our Lady of Antiquity (**Nuestra Señora de la Antigua**) whose effigy is supposed to have accompanied the Catholic monarchs when they captured Granada, and that of Jesus of Nazareth which has an ornate reredos. The elaborately carved and gilded organ is also a notable feature of the cathedral.

Once mass, which is always well attended at all Granada churches, is over the Plaza Alonso Cano in front of the Cathedral becomes a great gathering place as friends meet to exchange greetings, offering a glimpse of a complete cross-section of Granada's population, from the elegantly dressed middle classes to the always well-turned-out but less affluent, who also take pains to present a good appearance. Moving amongst them there are always the ubiquitous gipsy women offering a carnation for 'Amor' not 'dinero,' Only the very soft-hearted or very foolish accept this apparently generous gesture for to do so means being subjected to a moral blackmail that can only be halted by handing over the inevitable coin that the gipsy sought in the first place.

At the entrances to most churches in Granada, as elsewhere in Spain, beggars wait patiently – young girls, old women and mothers with babes in arms, but unlike the gipsies, these sit passively with hands outstretched and anyone inclined to a gesture of charity need not fear further importuning.

● The Royal Chapel

The spiritual heart of all Spain lies in the Royal Chapel (**Capilla Real**), adjoining the cathedral, for here lie the tombs of the monarchs of the Reconquista. The chapel itself is an airy place with Gothic vaulting and one of those solid gilded reredos of Hapsburg origin that can be found in most churches of Spain. At the entrance to the chancel is a magnificent wrought-iron gate and beyond it lie two magnificent marble tombs, built in tiers and with baroque decorations. On the top of one are the carved marble figures of Ferdinand and Isabella and on the other (artistically better) are their daughter, Juana la Loca and her husband, Philip the Handsome.

Unfortunately, the prone figures are at such a height that it is impossible to see them properly, except for Juana la Loca whose face, seen in profile, suggests the kind of tense, over-sensitive person that inevitably becomes a victim when faced with the harsh realities of life.

Steps leading down under the tombs enable visitors to gaze on the unadorned coffins in which the bodies of Ferdinand, Isabella, Juana and Philip lie.

In a room adjoining the chapel are relics of Ferdinand and Isabella, his sword and her sceptre and crown and the illuminated missal which she carried on all her campaigns. There are also some fine paintings in the room, notably a **Descent from the Cross** by Dierck Bouts and another **The Holy Women** by Memling.

There are many busy streets around the cathedral, including the narrow Alcaicería, once a silk market but now full of tourist souvenirs, and Pescadería which runs from the Plaza de Bibarrambla to the densely wooded Plaza Trinidad. The area has a small market and several restaurants, notably Cunnini fish restaurant in Pescadería, and a popular tourist restaurant, Sevillanos, with tables in the open. There are also excellent restaurants in Calle Duende, down Acera del Darro, a continuation of Reyes Católicos. Try Salvador restaurant for a down-to-earth meal in a traditional ambience and the Taverna del Duende for a more up-market version.

North of the Cathedral, a walk along the Calle San Jerónimo brings you to another group of fine buildings. including the **Collegiate Church of San Justo y Pastor**, the **Church of Iglesia del Perpetuo Socorro** and the church of **San Juan de Dios** which adjoins the hospital on whose a handsome patio you may see nurses in smart white trousers and overalls going about their work.

Further north is the University city, the apartment blocks of modern Granada and also the bull ring and football stadium. In contrast, you will also find in this part of Granada the baroque showpiece of the 16th century **Carthusian monastery, (Monasterio de la Cartuja).** Though the outside is plain, the interior displays the ultimate example of elaborate decoration of the kind one finds in Austria and southern Germany, overwhelming but also impressive in its way.

Near Granada, on the Cordoba road, is Fuente Vaqueros, a small village that is the birth place of possibly the greatest Spanish poet of this century, Federico Garcia Lorca. He was a literary radical, a playwright, a poet and was not acceptable to the Franco regime so he was shot. Today, his genius is well recognised and the village maintains a museum of his relics and works.

The Costas of Andalucía

Half a century ago the coast of Andalucía from the Portuguese frontier to Almería was a thinly populated stretch of rocks and scrub. Here and there in the valleys farmers struggled for a living and on the shores were tiny fishing villages with old, battered boats drawn up on the shore where during the day black-clad women patched and mended tattered nets. It was very picturesque, but the inhabitants lived without running water or sewage and in poverty. Their children playing barefoot in the streets, unless they left home for life in the cities, were destined for the same life as their parents. Today, the famers and fishing folk, or their descendants, have most of the conveniences of modern life, including cars, freezers and television sets and they shop at supermarkets. Their children go to school and some to University and the old life has gone for ever, much to the regret of sentimental visitors who regret the passing of what seemed to them a simple and true life.

Not many of those who live on the Costa del Sol regret the change that has come over their homeland, however, though some wonder how long the good times will last.

Most of the Costa del Sol is now a built-up area, barely a mile deep from the coast. Along the tourist strip the buildings rise five, six, eight, ten storeys high, interspersed with mass entertainment centres, aquaparks, fairgrounds, mini-golf courses, and lushly green full size golf courses, car race tracks and tennis clubs, all threaded together by highway E26 which a local taxi driver warned me not drive on as it was the 'carretera de la muerte' – Death Highway. In high summer the death is more likely to be a thrombosis than a violent one but either way it is not pleasant road to drive on, especially between Málaga and Algeciras.

Málaga is the capital of the Costa del Sol and its new–found wealth is creating a whole new town of modern buildings around the Plaza de la Marina where the wooded Alameda Principal and Paseo Parque meet.

189

It has its older part, though. The cathedral, reached through Calle Molina Larios, is a vast building started in the 16th century and contains the figures of Ferdinand and Isabella praying. More interesting is the Moorish Alcazaba which has a charming garden and now houses the Archaeological Museum. On the 440 ft hill above the Alcazaba is the Gibralfaro, or castle of the lighthouse, which is reached by a narrow wooded winding road which provides fine views of Malaga, shared by the Gibralfaro Parador on the Hill.

East of Malága the road winds along spurs of hills and cliffs, past **Nerja** which has a parador and **Almuñecar** and its high rise blocks to **Motril** then past the market gardens which grows crops for the north European markets. The plastic covering on the vegetables making the area look like a vast encampment.

The N340 coast road ends at **Almería** where the harbour is busy with ships loading fruit and vegetables and minerals from the inland mines. This part of Andalucía is desert dry and famous inland as a location for westerns, whose movie set towns are as deserted and ghostly as the real ones in Arizona but we will describe the region in the chapter on Valencia and the south east.

Atlantic Andalucía

From the Portuguese border to Gibraltar the Atlantic waves wash over 130 km of almost empty coast except for the ports of Huelva and Cádiz. Recently named the Costa de la Luz this neglected part of Spain hopes to become yet another of the holiday costas which now fringe almost the entire Iberian peninsula.

Though ignored for generations this coast has a long history beginning with the arrival of the trading Phoenecians. Later the Romans used Cádiz as a port but then it, and the whole region, languished until Columbus set off from Puerto de Palos, near **Huelva,** on his voyage of discovery. After that Huelva became for a while the most important port in Andalucía until it lost its leading role to Cadiz and Seville. In the 19th century its fortunes revived however with the arrival of English mining companies who began to exploit the copper found along the Rio Tinto.

Today the Huelva region looks to a new future in tourism for it is blessed with sandy beaches from the River Guadiana to the River Guadalquivir along the banks of which is the vast 80,000 hectare nature reserve of Doñana (Parque Nacional de Doñana). Here, there is a flourishing wild life of mammals such as wild boar, deer, otters, badgers etc and of birds including the millions that migrate annually to and from Africa.

To the south of the Guadalquivir is **Cádiz,** a port since the time of the Phonecians, which stands on a rocky bastion jutting out into the sea at the end of an isthmus.

This famous port has a rich and active history particularly of the period after the discovery of America and during the maritime struggle for command of the Atlantic routes during the 16th to 18th century. In 1587 Cádiz was surprised by Sir Francis Drake who made a raid on the Armada and in 1596 the port was sacked by the Earl of Essex and Lord Howard of Effingham. In the 17th century however Cádiz defences repulsed a series of attacks and was considered such a safe port that it acquired monopoly rights for the Spanish American trade and became extremely wealthy. In the 19th century Cádiz witnessed the departure of Admiral Ville-neuve for what turned out to be the most decisive sea battle of the 19th century-Trafalgar.

The great maritime events have left few relics in the ancient port, though much of the defensive ramparts remain. However, the atmosphere of the narrow streets with their old houses, the quayside bars, the excellent restaurants that offer the fish brought in by the fishing fleet and the activity of the busy harbour evoke memories of the role that Cadiz has played in the history of the sea.

Some relics can be seen in the museums of History and Archaeology and Art which contain finds from as early as the Phoenecian period and models of the port during its great days.

Inland from Cádiz lies **Jerez de la Frontera,** a town which grew during the 18th century when the wars against the

French forced English shippers to seek other sources of wine than Bordeaux. The importation of wine from what was then called Xeres led to the adoption of the name sherry for the famous aperitif. (See the Wines of Spain).

There is more to Jerez than sherry as all lovers of horses and horsemanship will know for it is also a famous breeding place of thoroughbred horses; and incidentally of bulls for the corridas. In May the famous Feria del Caballo (Horse Fair) attracts as many visitors as the Wine Harvest Festival in September and there is much spectacle and dancing of Flamenco and, of course, sherry drinking during both occasions.

Visitors interested in architecture find several buildings worth looking at in Jerez. Two of these are churches with Mudéjar towers one dedicated to St Saviour (**San Salvador**) and the other to St Michael (**San Miguel**). One with a particular attraction for horse lovers is the Chartreuse of Our Lady of Defension (**Cartuja de Nuestra Señora de Defension**) which has a splendid entrance facade and was noted for its stud farm, which unfortunately the monks were obliged to relinquish.

The east bank of the Guadalquivir was of course a frontier between Christian and Moorish Spain for many years and it is not surprising that so many of the towns in the region have the suffix 'Frontera' added to their names, among them are **Chiclana de la Frontera, Concil de La Frontera, Verger de la Frontera** and **Arcos de la Frontera** which is dramatically situated on the slopes of a giant crag by the Guadalete river. This splendid little town has a fine parador, the **Casa Nacional del Corregidor,** once a Jesuit headquarters.

All this region was the property of the Dukes of Medina Sidonia who were a power in the land at the time of Isabella and Ferdinand and whose ancestor Alonzo Perez Guzman, known as the Good, built the castle at Tarifa (the most southerly point in Spain) from which he defied the Moors who had his son as a hostage. Like the more recent but no less legendary Colonel Moscardo of the Alcazar at Toledo he prepared to sacrifice his son rather than surrender.

Tarifa lies 22 km from Algeciras, busy harbour which

looks across at Gibraltar waiting perhaps for the day when it will once more belong to Spain. The Moors arrived in Algeciras in 711 and departed from Spain in 1492 and the English arrived in Gibraltar in 1704 when Admiral Rourke captured the Rock, but when and if they depart is a problem that embarrasses two friendly nations.

Motoring itinerary

Day 1	Seville	
	Carmona	33 k 20 m
	Ecija	54 k 33 m
	Córdoba	51 k 31 m
	Total	138 k 86 m

Leave Seville by the airport road turning off along NIV also called E25 for Carmona/Cordoba. The road is good but busy because it is also the Madrid highway as far as Linares. There is a Parador in a formidable castle at Carmona. At Cordoba the Parador Nacional La Arruzafa is outside the town (3 k). It is modern with a swimming pool. Tel 275 900. In the town there is the Melia Córdoba, Jardínes de la Victoria Tel 47 31 42

Day 2	Córdoba	
	Linares	104 k 75 m
	Ubeda	26 k 16 m
	Baeza	9 k 5 m
	and back to Ubeda	9 k 5 m
	Total	148 k 92 m

Stay on the NIV as far as Linares and then continue along N322 to Ubeda. The N321 takes one to Baeza and back. The Parador del Condestable Dávalos at Ubeda is a lovely Renaissance building on the elegant Plaza de Vasquez de Molina. Tel 750 345

Day 3	Ubeda	
	Jaén	57 k 35 m
	Granada	97 k 60 m
	Total	154 k 96 m

The Parador Nacional de San Francisco is in the gardens of the Alhambra an old monastery. It is very difficult to reserve rooms here, so it is a matter of luck. Tel 221 440. Alternatively, there is the Alhambra Palace Hotel, mock Moorish but with a superb view over the city. Peña Partida. Tel 22 14 68.

Day 4	Granada		
	Antequera	108 k	67 m
	Ronda	83 k	52 m
	Total	191 k	119 m

For Granada take the N342 to Antequera. There is a good modern parador if you feel like breaking the journey. The state of the road from Antequera to Ronda is variable but a reasonable average speed of 30mph is possible as there is very little traffic. From Antequera take the N334 and after about 5 k turn off along the N342 to Campillos where one turns left along the N341 for Ronda. The Hotel Reina Victoria is in the style of its name and has a superb view over the gorge. Calle Jerez Tel 871 240.

Day 5	Ronda		
	Arcos de la Frontera	90 k	56 m
	Jerez de lax Frontera	23 k	14 m
	Cádiz	39 k	24 m
	Seville	123 k	70 m
	Total	270 k	165 m

The C339 from Ronda becomes the N342 which takes one to Arcos de La Frontera. There is a good Parador here, the Casa del Corregidor, once a Jesuit coach house. The road is secondary but reasonable. On reaching the motorway at Jerez de la Frontera you can use it or continue along the national road NIV for some 30 k to Cádiz. There is a motorway from Cádiz to Seville.

For an expensive treat stay at the Alfonso XIII, a Moorish style palace, Gran Via 668 Tel 318 52 00 About £50 a night. Otherwise there is the Doña Maria, Calle Don Remondo, near the Giralda. Tel 224 990 at half the price.

Chapter Nine:
The green hills of Spain

The mountainous land of north-west Spain is home to a diverse people of different origins: the Navarrese, the Basques, the Asturians and the Galicians, each proudly independent and maintaining traditions whose origins are sometimes difficult to trace and inhabiting Navarre, Euskadi, (the Basque country), Cantabria, Asturias and Galicia.

Geographically, the extension of the Pyrennean chain westwards to the broken Atlantic coast of Galicia has created a many-faceted land. Everywhere, mountains dip their feet into restless seas and raise their rocky heads to height of more than 2500 m (8000 ft). This high barrier between the seas and the arid plateau of central Spain catches most of the moisture carried in by the prevailing south-west winds, making this the greenest part of Spain and the coolest in summer, when people flock from the oven of Madrid to seaside resorts like San Sebastian and Santander.

Not that this is one of the mass sunbathers' Costas of Spain, though the beaches surrounded by green hills are superb. Rather, it is a land full of peculiar interest and mystery. As you drive along the narrow, twisting roads, deep in wooded ravines or high along corniche roads you discover a difference from the rest of Spain, a world related more to the Celtic fringe of Scotland, Wales, Cornwall and Brittany than to the Mediterranean. It is difficult to believe, except in the large urban connurbations of Bilbao and Santander and the port of San Sebastian, that this is also the most industrialised part of Spain for the folds of the mountains hide the factories, coalmines and steel works. It is quite a

195

surprise to emerge from a mountain pass into a narrow valley crammed with paper mills, chemical works, timber yards and the utilitarian apartment blocks in which modern Spain houses its workers. The main impression one obtains driving around this region is of a green landscape, of high peaks, especially in the Picos de Europa area, of rushing torrents where patient fishermen cast their flies for salmon trout and of little farms clinging tenaciously to steep slopes and, of course, of the sea rolling into narrow steep-sided coves or green, hilly inlets. North-west Spain is an ancient region, with Stone Age people leaving the marks of their presence in countless caves, the most famous of which is Altamira, westwards from Santander. The Celts settled here, and so did the mysterious Basques who can be found in Navarre and La Rioja as well as in the true Basque lands of Euskadi, and the Asturians and Galicians of Iberian stock.

When the Roman Empire of Spain decayed and the Visigoths moved the people of north west Spain withdrew into their mountains to resist the invaders, as later they would resist the Moors. The legendary King of Austurias and guerrilla leader, Pelayo, won the first victory over the Moors on Iberian soil at Covadonga in 722.

Despite its geographic and ethnic isolation from the rest of Spain, the North-west has been the location of many key events of Spanish history. Its mariners, who from the earliest times fished off the Newfoundland banks, helped to crew the ships that sailed to the New World and returned laden with the treasures of the Americas, bringing them to La Coruña and other Galician ports. The same expertise was put to the service of the Armada, which included a fleet from the North-west; and from the region's ports ships sailed to the northern ports of the Hapsburg Empire.

When Charles V himself first came to Spain to claim the throne, he entered the country at Villaviciosa. More recently, the North-west region also saw some of the more ferocious attacks of Franco's soldiers, who massacred Asturian miners in 1934 and destroyed Guernica in 1936.

The land of the Basques

The origin of the Basques, their language and traditions has long been a subject for debate among learned professors, but none has yet put forward a theory of their origins with which everyone can agree. Nevertheless, the Basque is unmistakable among Spaniards, even when he is not wearing the large flat-topped black beret which was once the universal symbol of Basqueness.

An observant visitor to the land of the Basques will soon discover some of the main characteristics of the Euskadi, (the land of the Basques.) First of all, in the streets of every city and village there is the evidence of the living Basque language on every sign.

San Sebastian is 'Donostia', Pamplona is 'Iruña', Vitoria is 'Gasteiz', and so on. Restaurants have names like 'Rekondo', 'Arzakor', and the white wine of the region is 'Txakoli'. On shop fronts or the brass plates of offices you come across such sonorous names as Irruretagoyena, Errazuriz, Echevarría and if you listen carefully you can hear the sharp staccato sound of the Basque language which often suggest that people are quarrelling when in fact they are having a friendly discussion.

The Basques have fought hard for their national rights or 'fueros'; and one of these, visible in every town and village, is the right to have their own police force which is easily identified by its red berets.

Even in such international resorts as San Sebastian, the Basque people stand firmly by their rights and identity. On a recent visit to the city during the 1988 August Festival I read in the Basque newspaper a long discussion about whether the entertainments was planned with the visitors or the Basque people in mind. In conversation with a resident of San Sebastian to whom I spoke about the great achievements of Euskadi in industrial development, I was reminded that the Basques still had certain rights, abolished by Franco, to recover. He was not however pinning his faith on ETA, the militant arm of Basque separation, for whom neither he nor others seemed to have much admiration.

● Jai Alai

The most Basque of all activities is the fast, exciting game called **Jai Alai** or pelota Vasca and anyone who wants to understand the Basque people should visit a 'fronton', a long rectangular court enclosed on three sides but with one long side open to the tiers of spectators who crowd the benches. Jai Alai has various forms, played either with the hand as in fives or, best of all, with a long curving basket (chistera) attached to the wrist which gives the ball an amazing force and speed. The courts, or 'cancha', can vary in size according to the game played. The most spectacular form of the game is the Rebote played with the chistera on a court of 100 metres (109 yards) long and 16 m (17.5 yds) wide. Thirty-two metres (35 yards) from the end wall is the Paso line which separates the area occupied by the attacking team at the rear end of the cancha or court and the defenders nearest the wall against which the ball is bounced.

The object of the game, which demands high standards of agility and stamina, is to keep the ball in play with both attackers and defenders hurling the ball against the end of other walls and trying to outwit their opponents. Scoring is as in tennis.

For spectators, the fun of the game is enhanced by gambling, which is conducted in a most remarkable manner. In front of the tiers of spectators the game's equivalent of a bookie standards with his hands and pockets full of slit tennis balls. As soon as any spectator shows any interest in placing a bet he is thrown a ball in which he inserts his bet. The betting balls fly to and fro throughout the game, odds change as the fortunes of the teams fluctuate and how it is all settled in the end is beyond this spectator's comprehension.

Jai Alai players are mostly professional and the gambling stakes for the game, which arouses intense enthusiasm throughout the Spanish-speaking world, runs into billions of pesetas. The Basque is an inveterate gambler as well as a devoted fan of physical prowess and skill.

● Basque gastronomy

Another typically Basque occupation is eating and it is claimed that the best food in Spain is to be found in **Euskadi.** Many of the dishes are based on the product of the sea and include such by now world-famous exotica as baby octopus in their ink (chipironeś en su tinta), bacalao al pil pil (deliciously prepared dried stewed cod) txanguro (spider crab) and other specialities of which top restaurants will not reveal the secret. Secrecy is, in fact, another Basque characteristic as far as food is concerned. Some of the best restaurants are hidden away on the first floors of buildings and behind doors opened only to customers who have made reservations. Try Nicolasa, 1st floor Aldemar 4 or Urepel on Paseo de Salamanca 3. Here you will find the menu will be full of dishes special to the house and the atmosphere more that of a select club than of a public eating place. To carry this a stage further, there are private eating clubs with an exclusive male membership who take it in turns to prepare their special menus; a mere stranger is unlikely to see the inside of these unless he has a very good Basque gourmet friend.

San Sebastian

In San Sebastian I came across some faded 1920s photographs in which the elegant resort was described as the Brighton of the Basque coast. This seemed an unlikely comparison until I remembered that San Sebastian and Biarritz, across the border in France, were sophisticated resorts between the wars, attracting not only the British aristocracy but also the well-to-do of all the courts of Europe. Some of the first international tennis, golf and motor racing championships were held here.

Something of this between-the-wars flavour still lingers at San Sebastian which has the most beautiful bay of any holiday resort in Europe with its two sandy beaches embraced by the hills which rise to the green humps of **Monte Urgull** and **Monte Igueldo.**

The main town lies between the River Urumea and the bay. It has some elegant streets with a few amusing art deco buildings as well as a number with the kind of spires and turrets which evoke the flamboyant style of Spanish Gothic architecture. The Avenida de la Libertad is the main boulevard, with cafés at the seaward end, though few fashionable shops, which, in San Sebastian, seem to be scattered all over the town. A fine promenade stretches along the **Playa de la Concha** and curves westwards along the smarter **Playa Ondarreta,** most of it lined with large apartment blocks. Between the beaches is the Miramar Palace, once the summer residence of the Spanish Royal family from the times of Queen Maria Cristina, who is commemorated in the very fine five star hotel, recently totally renovated, on the Paseo de la Republic Argentina.

The **Paseo de la Concha** is one of the centres of social life in San Sebastian. Here you can mingle with strolling crowds, vendors of jewellery and trinkets and fortune tellers, who are not the traditional head-scarfed gipsies, but young men in business suits who deal with the anxieties and hopes of their customers with the professional manner of a psycho-analyst.

Another centre of the social life of San Sebastian is in the old town which, in fact, is no older than the 1820s. When Wellington's troops arrived here, under General Graham in pursuit of Joseph Bonaparte's army during the Peninsular War there was one of those terrible explosions of savagery that ended with the murder of many of the men, women and children of the town and the destruction of the buildings.

Today, the ochre-coloured buildings of the old town huddle under Monte Urgell between the bay, where is a harbour for fishing boats and a string of fish restaurants under arcades, and the River Urumea. The grand buildings are the Town Hall (**Ayuntamiento**), once the Casino; the **Church of Santa María** which has an amazingly ornate entrance and many decrepit but once grand altarpieces inside; and the **Museum of San Telmo,** once a monastery. The main reason for visiting the old town is not for its monuments but for the life which surges through its narrow streets at the evening hours. As in most of Spain, in a San Sebastian the population crowds into the streets of the old quarter between 7pm and 10pm for the ritual of the evening paseo (stroll). In the few streets that form a grid round the **Plaza de la Constitucíon,** once used as a bullring, one can see all San Sebastian, rich and poor, the old and those in baby carriages, respectable families and hippies, the last behaving in a way that would not have been tolerated a few years ago. Everyone jostling each other in the bars and consuming large quantities of prawns, spiced sausages, fried squid and other delicacies as they wait for the restaurants to open around 10 pm. When these do open there are instantly queues at the most popular ones, though if you make it clear you are going to eat à la carte you may find yourself quietly escorted to an empty table, where you are likely still to be sitting past midnight, enjoying a Pacharán liqueur or one of the many liqueurs with French names produced in Spain under patent.

The French frontier lies a mere 10 km eastward from San Sebastian along a hilly coast with inlets containing busy dock area and some picturesque old villages, like **Pasajes de San Juan.** Near the frontier town of Irun is the peninsula on which lies **Fuenterrabia (Hondarrabia),** an ancient town which has become very fashionable because of its good beaches and picturesque buildings, now renovated and flower-bedecked in summer. For many touring visitors the attractions of Fuenterrabia include the opportunity to stay at the Parador of the Emperor Carlos V, a formidable stone fortress, the interior of which has been decorated with banners and tapestries but retains the austere and menacing atmosphere of a medieval stronghold. To stay here is positively an experience that leaves a powerful imprint on imaginative minds.

West of San Sebastian the coast continues its wayward line, with jutting headlands and steep-sided inlets, giving the motorist a slow but interesting journey to **Bilbao** and **Santander,** both important ports and industrial centres. A motorway now runs almost to Bilbao, but it is more rewarding to take the coast past the little resorts of Guetaria, Zarauz, Deva, Ondarroa and to enjoy the wonderful views of the coast and the Bay of Biscay. Beyond these lies the illfated **Guernica** which has been rebuilt and has therefore little of interest except for the tree of Guernica, an ancient oak, a descendant of the one where for centuries the great feudal lords, including Queen Isabella, swore to protect the rights of the Basque people.

Into Cantabria

Santander is a busy port built along a broad estuary. Though it has a cathedral and several museums it is visited more for its **El Sardinero** resort, which became popular between the wars when the Spanish Royal family took to frequenting the summer palace built for them by the town, perhaps in rivalry with San Sebastian with which Santander still competes by staging a summer festival.

Nearby to the west is the extraodinarily well preserved village of **Santillana del Mar** which is full of houses built by Spanish grandees who came here on pilgrimages to the shrine of Saint Juliana. One of these, once owned by the Barreda family, is now the **Parador Gil Blas,** named after the picturesque character from the novels of the French writer, Le Sage. Inland from Santillana are the famous caves of **Altamira,** discovered in 1897 but now only open to small numbers of the public due to the damaging effect of the humidity caused by the breath of visitors. Permission to visit must be obtained from the Centro de Investigaciones of Museo de Altamira, Santillana del Mar.

The country here is extremely hilly, rising to the **Picos de Europa,** an amazing mass of mountains going up to 2648 m (8688 f) in a matter of 30 km (20 miles) from the sea. There are three main blocks of mountains topped by sheer limestone crags which make for spectacular scenery as they rise out of the grassy and pine-forested lower slopes. At the eastern end is the Andara Massif, in the centre the Naranco de Bulnes Massif, and in the west the Covadonga Massif. You can drive between the massifs from Panes, to Cangas de Onis off the E50 road from Santander, in about 6 hours. The first stage, from Panes to Potes is about 27 km (17 miles) and takes you through the narrow La Hermida gorge. At Potes a side trip up the Deva river valley to Fuente Dé takes you into high mountain country where there is winter skiing and the cable cars continue to operate in summer so you can enjoy viewpoints.

From Potes, the road continues south over two passes to Riano, here you may turn north along a narrow road to the Ponton Pass and down to the gorges of the Sella River which are particularly dramatic at the point where the Ponga River meets the Sella. You then follow the Sella River valley to Villanueva where you can turn right for a return to Panes.

The total distance of the drive is 233 km (145 miles) and during its course you will see a superb variety of spectacular scenery.

Asturias

To the west of the Picos de Europa lies the old Asturian capital of **Oviedo,** the centre of which is occupied by a large park (**Parque de San Francisco**) and its adjoining old quarter. Most of Oviedo is of recent construction, having grown as the coal industry in the interior of Asturias began to be exploited in the 19th century. Much of the old town was destroyed during the rising of the miners in 1934 and the Civil War in 1936-37, when the Asturians remained loyal to the Republican government.

The Gothic cathedral, **Sancta Ovetensis,** at the centre of the old quarter in the Plaza Alfonso II has a 270 ft tower, one of the best Gothic campaniles in Spain. Its soaring lines are echoed in the cathedral itself which has a four-storey painted and gilded altarpiece above which rise the stained glass windows of the apse which contains a huge painted and gilded reredos. The original cathedral, built by Alfonso II, called the Chaste, remains in the Sacred Chamber (**Camera Santa**) which has some fine carvings of the apostles and contains treasures such as the cross worn by King Pelayo when he defeated the Moors at Covadonya.

Oviedo has several interesting churches of the period between the Visigoth occupation and medieval Romanesque and for anyone interested in this form of architecture a visit to **Monte Naranco** is essential. Personally, I find the simple, chunky architecture of the Romanesque period, of which there are two fine examples at Monte Naranco, more moving than the more expert and sophisticated Gothic style. **Santa María de Naranco,** which was built as a palace for King Ramiro I, did not become a church until the 13th century. The three storeyed building has a central hall with band vaulting and columns open at one end with three large rounded arches. The decorations are simple but beautiful and the proportions delight the eye as much as the panorama of Oviedo and the distant peaks of the Picos de Europa.

The second Romanesque church of Monte Naranco is **San Miguel de Lino,** a square chunky building which suffered from an earthquake in the 13th century but was restored to its original form. The interior still contains original relief carvings and old wall paintings.

From Oviedo to the coastal town of **Gijon** is 17 km (11 miles) by a motorway much used by the people of Oviedo whose patronage has made Gijon a fine seaside resort with an August festival which rivals those of other north-west resorts and attracts hippies, itinerant vendors and entertainers who spend their summer touring around the region.

19th-century coal exports gave Gijon some importance as a port but, fortunately, the demands for dock space required the building of a new port at El Musel and Gijon escaped industrialisation. **San Lorenzo Beach** is the popular summer rendezous and for local colour people go to **Cimadevilla,** the fishermen's village where sea-going trawlers and offshore launches nudge each other in the harbour and the narrow streets are lined with fish restaurants and bars selling the potent Asturian cider. This old village climbing up the Santa Catalina hill was also a favourite leisure centre for the Romans to judge by the remains of the baths built in the time of Emperor Augustus.

The end of the earth

Finisterre, literally 'where the land ends', is the most westerly point in Spain, and its rugged dangerous rocks have always been both a hazard and a landmark for seamen. This is a legendary place, for under its heaving seas lies a sunken city, and beyond the horizon is the once unknown world of the Americas. Finisterre is a place of hard realities coupled with mysticism and in this it represents Galicia itself, the most isolated and most introspective region of all Spain.

Like other parts of north-west Spain, Galicia has its mysteries: the Celts settled here in 1000 BC and the name Galicia has evident links with Gaul and Wales yet the language has Roman origins. Although the Galicians are strongly attached to their land, they form the largest core of most Spanish emigrant communities overseas. The Galicians are farmers, making things grow on the steepest, most unpromising mountain slopes, yet they are also great seamen; they are practical and forthright and are also deeply religious.

In all these characteristics they have much in common with the Celts of Western Europe, the Scots, the Welsh, the Irish and the Bretons. They even have the bagpipes (Gaita) which appear at every festive occasion accompanied by a drum to provide music for dancing.

As you drive along the green hilly countryside of Galicia you are very much aware of the rugged, self-sufficent nature of its people. Tiny farms marked by stone walls grow almost every imaginable crop of temperate regions, and cylindrical hayricks built around a central pole whose top is sometimes decorated with a hat or head, show that most farmers raise a few head of cattle. The corn is kept in stone barns raised on stilts to protect the grain against moisture and rats, and wine produced from small vineyards is stored in barrels in cool cellars. The Gallegos (as Galicians are called) live simply but well, and the products of the land are supplemented by that of the sea (cod, hake, turbot, eels, lobster, mussels, squid, crab). Favourite dishes, like Caldo Gallego (vegetable soup) Empanada (pasties), Pulpo a la Gallega (octopus) and grilled sardines are always abundant. Because of the poverty of life on the farms, most Gallegos have moved to the coast where industry thrives in the estuaries (rias) that indent the coast. As in other parts of the north-west, industrial development is discreet and most of the coast is unspoilt and heart-wrenchingly beautiful with the Atlantic rolling in on the craggy cliffs or rising along the green hills of the esturaries.

On the north-west corner of Galicia are the two large ports of **El Ferrol** and **La Coruña.** El Ferrol, which still retains some of its medieval quarter, is a naval base dating back to the 18th century when Spanish warships were constantly at war with or allies of the French, British and Dutch in their efforts to protect their American Empire and trade. Its other claim to fame is that it was the birthplace of General Francisco Franco whose stubborness, toughness and secrecy were true Gallego qualities.

To the south of El Ferrol across the Ria de Belanzas is La Coruña, a port whose name is inextricably associated with the name of Sir John Moore who, having retreatred there during the Peninsular campaign pursued by Marshal Soult, was mortally wounded during a heroic defence:

'Not a drum was heard, not a funeral note, etc.' To the Spaniards, La Coruña is more associated with the Armada which sailed from here on 22 July 1588 and for the repulse of an English fleet under Sir Francis Drake, who was under orders to invade Spain and install a Portuguese pretender on the Spanish throne. The heroism of a women called Maria Pita, who gave the alarm, is commemorated with a plaque on her house at Calle Herrerias 24 and in the Plaza named after her.

Elizabethan and Napoleonic wars are only a distant memory in the busy seaport today. Its old town, an area of narrow cobbled streets, is on a rocky isthmus where the lighthouse of the Tower of Hercules (**Torre de Hercules**) is a reminder that the Romans were here in the second century.

The two main avenues of the town centre are the Calle Real and Andres, and looking towards the harbour is the Avenida de la Marina, a fine avenue lined with old houses which have miradors (glassed-in balconies) arising through each floor, a characteristic feature of all Galician seaside towns, designed to provide maximum sunshine while protecting the inhabitants from the cold Atlantic winds. La Coruña's beaches, **Playa de Riazor** and **Playa del Orzan,** lie on the western side of the isthmus and the busy port and industrial zone are on the east.

West of La Coruña lies the sinister sounding coast of death ('**Costa de la Muerte**'), a rough shore with pounding waves when the weather is bad, but otherwise hardly deserving of its name. At Finisterre the coast of the long green estuaries, the Rias, begin. In the north these are still rugged but as they near Portugal a pastoral landscape embraces the blue fingers of sea which penetrate into the land.

As the southern end of the Rias coast is **Vigo,** still an important fishing port and once one of the main ports for trade with the Spanish American Empire. Treasure ships were often waylaid offshore by English and Dutch privateers and in 1709 Vigo was briefly held by the English during the War of Jenkins' Ear, a conflict which broke out on the flimsy pretext that a Spanish Captain had cut off the ear of an English sailor but whose real raison d'etre was the privateering business.

☆ ☆ ☆ ☆ ☆

The road to Santiago

In the 9th century Europe had still hardly recovered from the shock of being invaded by Moorish armies which had penetrated as far as Poitiers before being stopped by Charles Martel in 732. News and ideas travelled slowly in those days but gradually the peoples of Europe became aware that the Moors were a threat to their whole way of life and that only a more unified Western world could prevail agains them.

The most powerful unifying agent was religion, Christianity against Islam, and when the relics of the apostle James were discovered in western Galicia, the only Christian corner of Spain at the time, a champion for the Christian cause had been found. Soon, St James had acquired the nickname Matamoros (Moor Slayer) and the peoples of Europe trekked to his shrine to pay tribute to his powers. To help the pilgrims on the way the monastic orders, especially the Benedictines and Cisterians, and the Knight Templars and other noble societies set up hospices and hospitals along the route.

207

Soon, as many as two million people were trekking annually along the pilgrimage routes. They came from Scandinavia, England, Germany and Italy arriving by land over the Pyrenees or across the sea to the ports of Galicia.

The overland pilgrims crossed into Spain by the Passes of **Roncesvalles** and **Somport** rather than by the coast route which was swampy and plagued by mosquitoes and insects and where there was a none too friendly reception from the Basques who had been exposed to less well meaning invaders for centuries.

In Navarre and Castile the pilgrims were welcome for, since Sancho the Great of Navarre, it had been the policy of the kings of kingdoms to encourge Christians from north of the Pyrenees and even to provide places where they could settle permanently and thus increase the Christian population.

Roncesvalles had always been a main route into Spain and was the pass where Charlemagne's forces had been massacred by the Basques despite Roland's magic horn. Most pilgrims climbing up to the broad pass were no doubt aware of its history for this episode had become a legend recorded in the medieval epic of the Chanson de Roland. Their welcome was warmer than the one reserved for Roland and after attending services at the church of Our Lady of Roncesvalles (**Nuestra Señora de Roncesvalles**) they were no doubt regaled with food and other comforts by the monks of the monastery founded in 1130 by Alfonso I who was known as the Battler. The modern pilgrim sees a Gothic edifice with a tall square tower the interior of which has solid stone colums holding up pointed arches which reach up to a colonnaded clerestory above which are round stained glass windows and next to it the steep roofed buildings of the old monastery.

Surprisingly the complex of buildings is set in a broad green valley very different to the narrow pass one where imagine Roland and his knights died in bloody battle.

Leaving Roncesvalles you drive down a winding road to Pamplona and on to join the other pilgrim route from Somporto, which lies to the east long the Pyrenees, at **Puente La Reina,** a handsome steep five arched stone bridge alongside a small village on the River Arga.

The **Somporto** Pilgrims had a longer but perhaps more rewarding road after their Pyrennean crossing. After passing the summit at Somporto they wended their way down to **Jaca** along the banks of the River Argon. Jaca, still retains much of the medieval atmosphere of the time of the pilgrims, its ancient buildings huddle around the 12th century Benedictine monastery (**Monasterio de Monjas Benedictinas**) which supplied refreshments, prayers and encouragement and below it the high arched stone bridge of San Miguel still provides a crossing over the River Aragon.

From Jaca the pilgrims went west along the present N240 with plenty of monasteries to see them on the way and which today provide stops of interest to the motoring traveller.

The first of these is the monastery at St John of the Rock (**San Juan de la Peña**) a Benedictine foundation whose church apses are partly carved out of a cliff that overhangs the woods around the church. A delightful spot and you can see why the kings of Navarre chose it as the headquarters for the meetings during which they planned their resistance to the Moors and which they made as a royal pantheon, which still contains some 27 sarcophagi. Apart from its setting the old church of San Juan has a wealth of carved capitals in the cloisters which look out over the green countryside. There is also a newer church of St John above the cliff, this one built in the 18th century is less interesting and suffered considerable damage at the hands of French troops during the Napoleonic Wars.

Further along the N240m lies the Monastery of St Saviour (**San Salvador**) at Leyre. Situated on a rocky hillside Leyre (as it is commonly known) was also refuge for the kings of the early years of the reconquest of Spain. The present buildings date from about 1000 when King Sancho the Great rebuilt the monastery after it was sacked by the Moors. Though abandoned in the 19th century the monastery has been restored and its splendid stone architecture and decorated colums make it a building of considerable interest.

After merging at Puente la Reina the pilgrim routes continue to **Estella,** a trading centre and colony for pilgrims, especially French ones who settled there. The 12th century church of **St Peter** was a centre for pilgrims and contains varous items of interest including a curious serpent column of interwining snakes, a Romanesque madonna and some fine cloister capitals. There are a number of churches in the town including St Michael (**San Miguel**), Saint Sepulchre (**San Sepulcro**) and St John the Baptist (**San Juan Bautista**) all founded in the 12th century.

After Estella the pilgrims no doubt looked forward to their visit to **Logroño,** the centre of the Rioja wine business. Pictures of jolly friars with red faces and boisterous peasants like those painted later by Rubens spring to mind. At Logroño hospitality and encouragement was provided by the priests of Saint Mary of the Palace (**Santa Maria del Palacio**) a church built on the foundations of the old palace of Alfonso VIII and later pilgrims would have seen the building of Saint Mary in the round (**Santa María La Redonda**) in the 15th century which had its baroque towers added in 1742.

From Logroño the modern motoring pilgrim might be tempted to take the road marked in red on the maps to Burgos but it is more rewarding to follow the pilgrim cross country on the N120 which goes to **Nájera** capital of La Rioja and the centre of much disputed frontier region between Navarre and Castile. Though there were constant skirmishes here the pilgrim was protected by Orders of Knights sworn to keep the pilgrim routes open and protected. A further protection was given by the spirit of hermit who having failed to enter the monastery of Millan de la Cogolla took up his solitary existence by the pilgrims road and helped to maintain it in good order persuading local people to build a bridge across the river Oca. On his death he was buried by the pilgrim route and continued to keep an eye on pilgrims welfare.

With our more sceptical and materialistic minds we can interpret the whole of the St James pilgrimage as a propaganda exercise, which no doubt it was, but it also satisfied some deep need in the people of Europe judging by the vast numbers that travelled over the route to Santiago. Those who believe that the spirit of people can continue to reside in places may feel something of the medieval pilgrimage spirit in **Burgos,** the first great city of the pilgrimage route.

Burgos was the capital of old Castile until 1492 and shows it by the splendour of many of its buildings. It was the birthplace of the national hero El Cid (see Valencia) and the headquarters of a more modern hero/villain General Francisco Franco who set up his provisional government in opposition to the Republican government of Spain here in 1936.

The outstanding building of present day Burgos is the **Santo María Cathedral** an impressive building whose spiky steeples and pinnacles in the Gothic flamboyant style dominate the city skyline. The interior of the cathedral is equally splendid though decorated in two distinct period styles, that of the 13th century in the nave, aisles and portals and the Capilla del Condestable in the 15th, the same century that saw the dramatic western spires by Juan de Colonia erected in the style of ship's mast with a lookout gallery near the summit. The chapel beyond the apse is wonderfully ornate in the Isabelline style and contains the tombs of the High Constable of Castile and his wife who lie before a sumptuous altar.

A simpler, but perhaps more noteworthy tomb, at least for those of a romantic disposition, is that of El Cid and his wife Jiména who lie under a plan slab in the choir which also possesses a superb gold trimmed lantern vault and some boisterous pagan carvings on the misericords.

The most striking feature of the interior is the extraordinary number and variety of the chapels grouped round the nave and cloisters. Nearly all of them are highly decorated and one of two are particularly memorable for their outré character. In the Capilla del Santo Cristo, for example the attempt to imbue the Christ figure with realism has led to the covering of the statue with real skin (probably buffalo hide though some believe it to be human) real hair and real fingernails. Another memorable figure is the devil that emerges from a hole high in the nave in order to strike the hours and is known as Papamoscas, the flycatcher.

Underneath the cloisters are yet other strange inhabitants of the church, these are the Gigantones, giant figures common to many Spanish towns which are carried out the streets at festival times.

Near the west door of the cathedral is the chapel of San Nicolas which has a splended altarpiece by Simon of Cologne (Simon de Colonia,) son of Juan (1505) and above it the hill with the ruins of the castle blown up by Napoleon in 1813. It was here that Edward I married his beloved Eleanor of Castile for whom on her death he raised memorial crosses at every stopping place of her body on its last journey in England.

The social centre of Burgos lies to the east at Plaza de José Antonio, pretty arcaded square, and beyond it is Calle Santander the main shopping street in which is situated the **Casa del Cordon,** the palace of the Constables of Castile and a prison of Juana La Loca while her husband, Philip and her father Ferdinand made a treaty to prevent her assuming her position as Queen of Spain; and the place where Philip later died. It was here also that Columbus was received after his second voyage to America.

The historical centre of Burgos was once defended by a wall above the River Arlanzon along the banks of which there now runs a busy avenue. Its main feature then as now is the magnificent **Arco de Santa María,** a gateway entrance to the city; on it among other notables are the figures of Charles V and El Cid.

For anyone interested in the relics of the history of Burgos since Roman times a visit to the Prehistoric and Archaeological and Fine Arts museums is illuminating. The museum is housed in two Renaissance houses (**Casa de Miranda and Casa de Angulo**) and contains Roman and Visigoth finds as well as works of art of the medieval and Renaissance periods.

The period during which the plans for the reconquest of Spain were gathering force is vividly evoked in two monasteries on the outskirts of the city, one to the west and one to the east.

The monastery to the east of Burgos is the **Cartuja de Miraflores,** a Carthusian monastery founded by Juan II father of Isabella, in whose reign the monastery was completed in Isabelline style. The exuberant decoration which characterised the architecure of the reign of the Catholic monarchs is a feature of the church which contains the work of Gil de Siloe who, with Simon de Colonia, was a protagonist of the new flamboyant style which expressed the confident and outgoing character of the reign of the monarchs who united Spain.

The Monasterio de las Huelgas Reales, to the west of Burgos, was founded by Alfonso VII, and his wife Eleanor daughter of Henry II of England, and was one of the most important Cistercian monasteries in medieval Spain. The royal couple are buried in the monastery church along with some sixteen Castilian royal and noble personages. Many of the tombs were opened after the Civil war and were found to contain items of clothing and decoration which had survived in almost perfect condition. These are now on display in a small museum where you can now examine the clothing and accessories of people who lived seven hundred years ago.

The monastery, which controlled over 50 towns in the region, was also the headquarters of the Knights of Santiago (St James the patron saint of the Reconquest of Spain) who received their knighthoods from a wooden effigy of the saint with a movable arm holding the sword which bestowed the accolade.

Leaving the monastery of Las Huelgas the pilgrims way enters the rolling landscape of the Castilian meseta which stretches to the horizon, beige in summer, with baked earth and the dried stalks of wheat and grass, and white with snow in winter. At **Castrogeriz** a castle rises on a hill above the plain and some 30 km further on another cluster of buildings break the flat infinity of the landscape. These are the remnants of the Church of **San Martin de Fromista** which was built alongside a Benedictine Monastery founded in 1035 by the widow of Sancho the Great. The church was much restored in the 19th century and many of its carvings date from that period but some of the original ones remain. **Fromista** is the village of St Elmo who had suffered martyrdom according to legend by having his intestines pulled out of him by a windlass. The connection with ships has made him a saint who looks after sailors on the Galician coast and the balls of light (caused by electrical discharge) which sometimes appear on masts of ships, or on trees and telegraph poles, are said to be evidence of his presence watching over people out in stormy weather.

Some 15 km beyond Fromista is the town of **Carrión de las Condes** (Carrion of the Counts) named after the warrior knights who lived by the river Carrion to protect the borders of Leon. The counts of Carrion were not above such earthly vices as greed and cruelty however as the story of El Cid's daughter shows (See Valencia). Little remains of the former glory of Carrion in the present town though the church of **Santa María de Carrion** still stands in the village square, its great square tower a reminder of its defensive role. The south portal has some Romanesque sculptures of good quality showing the Three Kings and the Old men of he Apocalypse and there are further carvings at the church of St James (Santiago).

From Carrion de Las Condes to **Leon** is 90 k, a long monotonous walk for the pilgrims though they could look forward to the hospitality of the most important city of Christian Spain which had increased in size owing to the influx of Mozarabs (Christians who lived in Moorish dominated Spain). Today, the Augustinian monastery which provided lodging for pilgrims is the city's superb parador Hotel San Marcos.

Leon remained little changed since the days of the pilgrims until the 19th century when the iron and coal in the region made it into a prosperous industrial city. Much of the ancient city remains however in the sector to the east, away from the River Bernesga, where some of the old walls encircle the **Cathedral of Santa María de Regla** and **Church of Saint Isidore.**

The cathedral built in the 13th and 14th centuries, and based on the plan of Rheims, is superb and unusual. Two great dissimilar towers flank the beautiful facade which has a large rose window above the three arch portico. The central portal is magnificent and rich with carvings as are the south portal and the northern one which opens onto the cloisters.

The interior is breathtaking with an amount of stained glass only equalled in French cathedrals. The choir, which as in most Spanish churches dominates the centre of the nave, has some lovely alabaster carvings, and there are some superb paintings including the 15th century altarpiece in the main chapel (Capilla Mayor) by Nicolas Frances who also painted some of the cloister frescos.

No less imposing, but in the Romanesque style, is the Collegiate church of **San Isidoro** on the western wall of the old town. This solid undecorated church inspires by its fine proportions and surprises by the tall scalloped arches which suggest the Moorish influence introduced by the Mozarab emigrants to the city. The church has some fine carved capitals and notable tympanum whose theme is Abraham sacrificing Isaac; the carving of the Lamb of God over the arch has given the portal the name of The Lamb portal. (**Puerta del Cordero**) The portal of the south transept is equally beautiful and is known as the Portal of Forgiveness (**Puerta del Perdon**) and features the Crucifixion.

San Isidoro was a pantheon of the early kings of Leon and there are 11 kings and 12 queens in the crypt which has many carved capitals and Romanesque frescoes.

Across the city by the river is another important building which was one of the features of the old medieval town, this is the Monastery of St Mark (**Antiguo Monasterio de San Marco**) once the headquarters of the Knights of the Order of Santiago who protected pilgrims on the route to Santiago de Compostella it became a monastery under the patronage of Ferdinand who was Grand Master of the Order. A visitor to Leon will also derive much pleasure from the old streets to the south of the Cathedral and around the Plaza Mayor and the Market place (**Mercado**) where ancient houses, little shops, and the market itself provide inumerable vignettes of life in this splendid old city.

From Leon the pilgrims began their ascent into the mountains that rise from Leon into Galicia. There were some sixty km to cover to **Astorga,** then a walled city with the 11th century church of Santa Maria at its centre. In the following years the church was rebuilt twice and the present one dates back to the 17th century when the two towers and the Plataeresque facade were created. The Bishops palace (**Palacio Episcopal**) is quite a different matter. This was built by Gaudi and is considered by some to be his best work. Here Gaudi seems to have deserted his inclination to use natural forms in his architecture and has produced a kind of legendary palace of the kind favoured by King Ludwig of Bavaria; an astonishing piece of work which today houses the Museum of the Pilgrims Way (Museo del Camino) which displays souvenirs of the Santiago pilgrims.

Beyond **Ponferrada,** 6 km away, pilgrims had once again a choice of routes, some going north to Lugo, and others taking a more southerly route via Puertomarin, a village which has since been drowned by the building of a dam across the River Mino. Its Church of the Knights of St John of Jerusalem still survives, though not on its original site, for it was moved stone by stone to a new location above the water level.

Those who went by **Lugo** found a city whose walls still surround its old quarter in the south of which is the cathedral of Santa María which began as a copy of Santiago de Compostela but ended up as a mixture of styles.

At **Santiago de Compostela** the pilgrims gathered in what is now the great Plaza de España, a magnificent open space overlooked by the 11th/13th century cathedral and numerous splendid houses, including the Bishops's Palace (**Palacio Gelmirez**). The impressive Spanish baroque facade of the **Cathedral** of Santiago with its two baroque towers, the Torre de las Campanas (bell tower) and Torre de la Carraca, was added later in the 18th century, by the architect Fernardo Casas y Nova, and is considered to be the best baroque church front in Spain. Medieval pilgrims did not see it, of course. Instead, they entered the Cathedral by the Portico de la Gloria which is a superb example of a 12th-century carved Romanesque doorway comparable to those found at Vezelay and Autun in Burgundy. Seated on a column before it is a statue of Santiago.

The interior of the Cathedral is also Romanesque and looks much as it did to the medieval pilgrims, though the sanctuary and some chapels have later decorations. The baroque Capilla Mayor houses reliquary of St James and the Capilla de la Reliquias has other holy relics including a tooth of the saint. There are many fine pieces of Sculpture in the cathedral and some superb wrought-iron work in the Mondragon chapel.

Beneath the cathedral are several crypts. One, at the Plaza de España entrance to the cathedral, contains the church that existed before the cathedral was built in the 12 century and excavations under the south transept have revealed a Roman necropolis which suggests that the name Compostela has a Latin origin, deriving from the word meaning cemetery.

Not unexpectedly, Santiago de Compostela has an abundance of churches and religious buildings. Among them are the Bishop's Palace (**Palacio Gelmirez**), which lies alongside the cathedral; the **San Martino Pinario Monastery,** where more work by Casa y Novoa can be seen in the reredos of the high altar; and the **Hospice of the Catholic Monarchs,** which has a very fine facade facing on to the Plaza de España. This building, originally built by order of Ferdinand and Isabella as a hospital and inn for pilgrims, today continues to dispense hospitality as a parador, the Hotel Reyes Católicos.

As we know from Chaucer's Canterbury Tales, pilgrims were not all that different from today's tourists and Santiago de Compostela catered for all their needs spiritual and material. Today the city maintains its traditional hospitality. Bars and restaurants are lively well into the early hours during the summer months, and even in winter for Santiago is a University City and has a youthful air about it. The Festival of St James takes place on 25 July and at that time accommodation becomes difficult to obtain.

☆ ☆ ☆ ☆ ☆

Motoring intineraries

Day 1	Santander		
	Bilbao	107 k	67 m
	Vitoria	65 k	40 m

Logrono	85 k 53 m
Total	257k 161 m

Leave Santander on the E50, also called N634. At Bilbao take N240 to Vitoria where you take the NI dual carriage way to the N232 Logroño exit. In Logroño there is the modernised turn of the century style Gran Hotel, General Vara del Ray 5 Tel 25 2100. Some 50 k further along the Zaragoza Road at Calahorra is the Parador Nacional Marco Fabio Quintillano, a modern parador named after the Roman elecutionist born here

Day 2 Logroño

Estella	47 k 29 m
Puente La Reina	14 k 8 m
Pamplona	24 k 15 m
Total	85 k 62 m

Logroño is the centre of the wine industry and there is a great temptation to wander around the small roads that connect the vineyards. Leave Logroño on the N III which goes all the way to Pamplona.

Day 3 Pamplona

Leyre (Sanguesa) to turning for Jaca	47 k 29 m
Jaca	59 k 37 m
Canfranc (frontier)	23 k 14 m
Pau (France)	98 k 61 m
Total	227 k 141 m

Leave Pamplona on the N240 which continues as far as the Jaca Road C134. For San Juan de la Peña Monastery it is better to go on to Jaca and approach it from the N330 which runs south from Jaca. From Jaca the N330 goes north to Canfranc and Puerto de Somfort at the frontier with France. After the first few hairpin bends the N134 is a good, easy road. At Pau there is a Mapotel called Continental, 2 Rue du Foch.

219

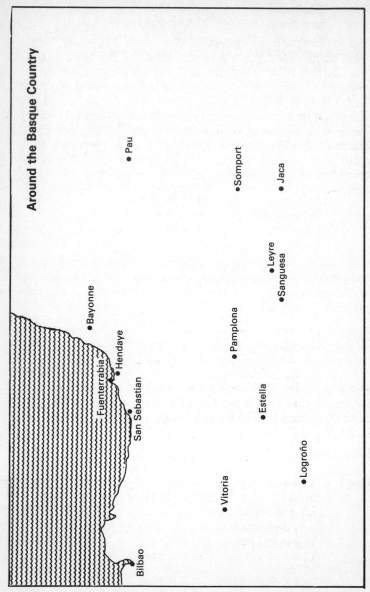

Around the Basque Country

Day 4 Pau
Bayonne	107 k 67 m
Hendaye	36 k 22 m
Fuenterrabia	10 k 6 m
(Hondarrabia)	
San Sebastian	21 k 13 m
(Donostia)	
Total	174 k 108 m

The Maria Christina is a top class hotel that has been
refurbished in the last two years. It is expensive, but well
worth it if you are in the mood for luxury. Paseo de la
Republica Argentina, Tel 426 770. Otherwise, try the
Londres y de Inglaterra, near the beach, Calle Zubieta 2.

Day 5 San Sebastian
Bilbao	via the motorway is 95 k	95 k 59 m
	via the coast is longer but more fun	107 k 67 m
Santander		
Total		202 k 126 m

To go by the coast road take the C 6212 to Guernica and then
the N634 which joins the E 50 to Santander. At Santander
you can stay at the El Sardinero resort. The Hotel Real,
Paseo de Perze Galdes 28, Tel 27 25 50 (open summer only)
is in a splendid old building and overlooks the sea. Or you
can go beyond Santander (24 k) to Santillana del Mar and
stay at the Parador Gil Blas, a lovely 15th noble house. Tel
81 80 00.

b)

Day 1 Santander
Panes	80 k 50 m
Side trip round the Picos de Europa to	
Cangas de Onis	142 k 89 m
Total	222 k 139 m

The trip round the Picos de Europe is superb and takes about five hours. Leave Santander on the E50 (N634) and turn left at Unquera for Panes on the N621 which climbs through the Hermida Gorge to Potes, then it continues through the San Gloria Pass to Riano. Here you turn north along the C637 to the Pandetrave Pass, where you'll find wonderful views, and down into the Sella valley. After two gorges the road comes to Cangas de Onis. There are one or two simple hostales at Cangas but the nearest hotel is the Pelayo at Covadonga, Tel 84 60 00. Take the C6312 eastwards for about 5 k and turn right up hill to reach the village.

Day 2	Cangas	
	Oviedo	76 k 47 m
	Canaro	91 k 56 m
	Ribadeo	71 k 44 m
	Total	238 k 149 m

The road from Cangas to Ribadeo is the E50 (N634) but it is worth making a detour to Gijon N 630 and driving along the coast on the N632. The roads meet at Canaro. At Ribadeo stay at Parador Nacional de Ribadeo, Amadro Fernandez Tel 110 825, which overlooks the sea. There is another parador at Villalba some 35 k further on in the former tower of the castle of the Counts of Villalba. Tel 51 00 11.

Day 3	Ribadeo	
	Barreiros	26 k 16 m
	La Coruña	136 k 85 m
	Santiago de Compostela	53 k 33 m
	Total	215 k 134 m

Leave Ribadeo on the E50 (N634) which runs all the way to La Coruña, thereafter continuing as E 50 but now N550, to Santiago de Compostela. Stay at the Parador Nacional de los Reyes Catolicos, a beautiful 15th century pilgrims hospice. Plaza del Obradoiro Tel 582 222.

Day 4	Santiago	
	Lugo	159 k 99 m
	Ponferrada	123 k 76 m
	Astorga	62 k 38 m
	Leon	47 k 29 m
	Total	391 k 244 m

A long day's drive across mountainous country starting on the C547 to Ponferrada and then on to the NVI to Astorga and the N 120 to Leon. The Hotel San Marcos was originally a monastery. Plaza San Marcos Tel 237 300

Day 5	Leon	
	Sahagun	68 k 42 m
	Carrion de las Condes	43 k 26 m
	Fromista	20 k 12 m
	Burgos	72 k 45 m
	Total	203 k 127 m

Stay at the Hotel Condestable Calle Vitoria 8, a fine traditional establishment or if you prefer a hotel outside the city there is the Landa Palace on the Madrid road. It is a mock medieval building with towers but contains genuine old furniture. Tel 20 63 43. Start from Leon on the N601 but turn off after 34 k towards Sahagun on the N120 which goes through to Burgos. the whole route is over the rolling plains of the Castilian mesta.

Day 6	Burgos			
	Santander	131 k 82 m	Total	131 k 82 m

An easy drive on the N623 over the Montes de Oca. For anyone who quails at the long coastal drive from Santander to La Coruna there is a pleasant alternative which is to travel on the Cantabrico railway tour. This takes 8 days on the FEVE narrow gauge railway and you sleep 7 nights on the train, which stops frequently to allow visits to the major towns.

223